Fifty-Two Weeks of Clarity

Fifty-Two Weeks of Clarity

How to Transcend to Self-Reliance

DR. JILL LEE

Fifty-Two Weeks of Clarity

Copyright © 2016 by Dr. Jill Lee

Published by:
Professional Woman Publishing
www.pwnbooks.com

ISBN: 978-0-578-18235-3

THE SPIRIT OF A DRAGONFLY

*The dragonfly is a symbol clarity and change and has been
thought to be the keeper of our dreams and aspirations. It is
considered by many cultures to be a symbol of harmony, prosperity,
and luck, representing all that is good. The dragonfly also
symbolizes purity, speed, and happiness.*

*The iridescent colors of its wings are like the colors of the Universe,
as they connect to everything and everyone. As the dragonfly
matures during its very short life, the colors of its wings change,
becoming more vivid and bright. A reminder that we can move
past self-created illusions and allow the change and
transformation of our lives to take place.*

*The spirit of the dragonfly reminds us to live
in the present moment, and live life to its fullest.*

*If you are lucky enough to have been visited by a dragonfly —
take heed. It's like a gentle breeze of awareness, reminding you
to look within…at that very moment.*

To my family — Life's greatest blessing —
Where we give and receive unconditional love —

Contents

Introduction

As I reflect on my own life, as well as my teachings, I realize that there are many ways to view life as we know it and life as we live it. There are many elements that can impact how we address each life situation and challenge that we may be confronted with. Can we see through our clouded vision or is it better with clarity? For me, I have found that I can navigate through life much better when I have clarity. And it is through this clarity, this book came to be.

Each chapter in this book is an insight to help you gain clarity. It's an opportunity to take each challenge, see it through a different lens and gain a diverse perspective; that which serves your well-being. You will begin to use your personal power to see and think "beyond the obvious." You may even find that you are bargaining with yourself, or asking *"What am I willing to give up for growth and change? How difficult can it be? What do I have to gain?"* When you stop, ponder and ask such questions of yourself, you may be very pleasantly surprised with your answers. This is when you begin to take responsibility for the life choices you make, and discover that these choices made today will affect how you live your life tomorrow.

When you change your thinking patterns, and how you look at life, you then change the way you live it. And it's through this diversity that you learn and grow. You can use each life experience to enhance your own reality, bringing balance to your mind, body, soul and spirit. Each shift that you encounter will bring about new beginnings, new experiences, and new opportunities.

Each week of the next fifty-two weeks is a chance for you to clear away toxic emotions while allowing you to discover and make room for your "Zen"…or your "Happy Place." You are freeing up your "inner mind space" and clearing away anything that may be blocking, crowding, or clouding your vision. It's an opportunity for you to live your best life while letting life touch you in the most beautiful ways.

During the course of writing this book, as much as I thought I knew about myself, I realized there was more. I have learned to listen to my own intuition, that voice inside my head that speaks without a sound… it's called inner guidance. We all have it; we just need to find moments of stillness so that we can listen. Through listening, you gain self-understanding, and you begin to hold yourself accountable for your choices. This is all part of learned self-discipline.

This is your personal journey. It's your life, and you are in charge. You own the choices you make. You've been given this gift of life… this gift of "now". There's no need for you to surrender to limitations. Live each day deliberately, with purpose and passion. Simply, effortlessly, and with clarity, embrace this time. Remind yourself to ask *"What if?"* instead of saying *"If only."*

This book offers you the opportunity to live an ordinary life, in an extraordinary way. Never stop learning and never stop growing. Let your ambitions be the food for your desires.

As we embark together on this journey of the next fifty-two weeks, let us keep our minds open, as well as our hearts, to receive and absorb the information provided in this book. Remember to "pause" and "ponder". We will feel through our emotions. Ask yourself "What do I need more of and what you need to release?" Search for the answers that will best serve your well-being. That which will bring the knowing of balance and of self-completeness into your life.

Let us begin.

WEEK ONE

Life is A Gift;
Living is an Art

Are you so consumed with the day to day rituals and responsibilities to realize what a gift you've been given? **The gift of life.** Yes…life is a gift, but how you choose to live it can be just like creating art. However; it's not so much about how the gift is packaged, it's more about the package itself.

We look at art and can appreciate the depths of inspiration and efforts that have gone into creating it, as it becomes something to be admired. You can apply the same inspiration, creating admiration and appreciation for your life.

When you are admiring a painting, you may see the colors, the technique, or only the image on the canvas. It gives you pleasure, amusement, even contentment. That in itself is a gift. It does not know that it has given anything to you, nor does it ask for anything in return. It just is. That is art. The same applies when you give your attention to someone; that is also a gift. It's how you **give your attention** that becomes art.

Life offers you the opportunity to make choices every day and the privilege to live your life to its fullest. That's not to say that there won't be days that seem more burdensome than others, but it's how you approach each challenge that makes the difference. Embrace and develop this life that you have been blessed with; and remember that art is not necessarily what you think you may see, but what you make others see. Live your life and let others appreciate the art in you.

***Ponder** — I see clearly that my gift of life is like art —*
How do I want others to see me?
Am I giving my full attention to others
when I am in their presence?
How can I appreciate the art of my life?

"And when there are times you are blessed
with a choice whether to laugh or cry —
Choose to laugh — it's good for the soul
and lightens the heart
Simplicity can fill your heart without words."

— DR. JILL LEE —

Listen to the Internal Calling of Your Heart

We all have an inner calling. Something that tugs or speaks to us from the depths of our heart. It's passion that whispers to you silently, through your feelings and emotions. But in order to hear, you must quiet your mind from all the chatter. Only then can you hear your heart speak. It's a special kind of listening. Don't ignore any signals that may beckoning for your attention.

When you speak aloud, you hear your words, but when you are listening to your inside voice, you can methodically hear and feel at the same time. Yes… you can feel your own voice and as well as your words. How often to you listen to what your heart is telling you? Your heart can reveal so much, and at the same, it allows you to tap into this internal calling. Only by **listening** can you seek the essence of your life. Only then will you know what lies at the bottom of your heart.

With this knowledge, your options are endless. You become emboldened. Acknowledge what you hear. Say it out loud. If you like what you hear, then allow it to become your passion. Allow it to become your purpose. Invite it in and feel the connection. On the other hand, if you don't like what you hear, you have options. You and only you can make changes in your life. Seek that which empowers you and gives you purpose. This will allow you to live your life with a happy heart, always in tune, and in balance with the whispers from your soul.

Ponder — I see clearly that I must listen
to whispers of my heart and soul —
What is my heart telling me?
Am I going to listen to my internal calling?
What are the choices I am presented with?

"At times, you may seem to ponder with worry —
but through the darkness — there is a light
that shines deep within your heart."

— DR. JILL LEE —

Expect Unexpected Challenges

At any given moment, when you least expect it, life can present you with all sorts of challenges. You have no time to prepare and no time think about how you might handle what's just come about. These challenges will test your courage and willingness to accept, adapt or modify.

If you're struggling with a situation, you can't pretend that it doesn't exist. You can't pretend that nothing has happened. You can't say, *"I'm not ready"* or *"wait, I need more time."* The challenge doesn't wait. It's there, right in front of you and it is your responsibility to acknowledge it now and address it as it arrives. Only then will you be able to work through it and make the necessary adjustments so you can move forward in your life.

You can't move backward to change an incident or situation. For this reason, you know what you have to do! ***You must accept the challenge!*** It's part of your journey. Loosen your grip and take hold of the situation gently and with confidence. Watch things unfold gracefully as everything falls into place.

Through courage and perseverance, you can see your way through any life situation. That's not to say it won't be difficult. Believe that your life matters. Believe that you are worthy to live a happy life. It is your birthright!

***Ponder** — I see clearly that I am worthy of a living*
a happy life, and I can confront
each challenge as it arrives —
What challenges am I faced with?
Will I accept the challenge?
What internal tools will I use to make the necessary changes?

"Some catastrophic moments invite clarity...
then explode in a single moment.
Be mindful...be aware."

— Dr. Jill Lee —

WEEK FOUR

Remove
Self-Created Illusions

As a dragonfly exhibits its iridescent transparency through its wings, it allows you to see its translucent colors. How do you show your colors, are they transparent? What do you see and what do you know for sure? Is what you see an illusion within yourself? The key word here is "illusion". Now…ask yourself, "What is transparent to me through my *own* illusions? The real discovery and awareness comes from recognizing what you see through your mind and felt with your heart. The knowledge you hold; once transparent; can be unmasked, identified and transformed into anything that you desire. Illusions are manifested to protect any weakness or fears, and you can ***remove anything negative*** that doesn't serve your well-being.

A self–created illusion is the same as self-deception. It can, at times limit and stifle your growth and cloud your clarity. It can alter your physiological mindset. It can alter what is true and what is real. You can decide whether to embrace and embellish what you see, or move into another direction. Only when you recognize this self-truth, can you remove these illusions and gain clarity in your life.

You can live your life with **clarity** by accessing these misconceptions and seeing them for what they truly are. Choose whether to embrace and embellish what you see or let it go and move into an entirely different direction that may serve you better in all aspects of your life. **You have the ability to soar** when you see things as they really are. It's wonderful when you know that the world can't interfere with what's inside of your head. So choose to be in love with your life, every moment of every day.

> ***Ponder*** *— I see clearly that I am worthy*
> *of being in love with my life every day —*
> *What do you know to be true? What do you see to be real?*
> *What can you feel that is honest?*
> *What illusions can you recognize and define?*
> *What illusions are you able to release?*

> *"Open your eyes and see — open your heart and feel*
> *Feel what you see — and see what you feel."*

> — Dr. Jill Lee —

The Effects of Chaos to Stress

You may never know when chaos sneaks up and enters your life. It's a gradual process, and before you realize it, you are confronted with turmoil all at once, like an explosion. Chaos can derive from many different things, such as outside forces or internal manifestations. Family related issues, personal relationships, and work related situations can also cause turbulence in your life. So what happens once you are confronted? Stress develops. The internal problems quite often evolve into chaos and vice versa. When it arrives, you are thrown right into the middle of it, and often, you didn't invite it in.

Now you are faced with a variety of symptoms. Anxiety, sleepiness, performance challenges, as well as conflicts in your relationships, not to mention health issues. Each situation differs with every person.

So often, you may try to hide behind the structure of these initial problems while attempting to sustain a calm state of being. Perhaps it's because you don't want others to know of this internal world wind of chaos. This is a very common way to protect yourself. Withholding is the minds defense. Fight it, freeze it, or flee it are all reactions. I am sorry to say, but there is no "One size fits all" solution.

Sooner or later you must access and assess the chaos. It is important to recognize the root of the stress in which this chaos was caused and how it's gotten out of hand. You must realize what's happening, and, as a result, there can be a shift in your behavior as well as your mood swings. There will be great diversity in the quality of your life. You will experience a transformation in your relationships, and you will enjoy a more balanced sense of well-being.

You may ask how? Well, you can accept or adapt to the situation. You can try to alter or even avoid the issue. If these solutions don't work for you, there is an alternative. You can seek help getting in touch with your emotions. The happy ones, the sad ones, as well as the difficult ones. It's about acknowledging, assessing and addressing each issue. See it for what it is. You can have renewed energy from gaining this clarity. Getting in touch with your internal self and getting right to the core will bring peace and harmony into your life.

Ponder — *I see clearly that I am able to address*
any chaos that enters my life —
How am I able to tap into my emotions?
How can I address this chaos before it evolves into stress?
Which internal tools can I use to uninvite chaos?

"Losing your balance is just part of life.
Keep your heart open and your mind unclouded."

— Dr. Jill Lee —

Learning To Cope

Not everyone gets "Happily ever after". Often, we are faced with situations or challenges that just come about and happen to catch us off guard. There are circumstances that may cause us to feel uncomfortable, anxious, and even fearful. I am not talking about physical challenges at the moment; I will address that in another chapter. I am, however, referring to your day to day situations.

Most often, our society is too quick to fix a problem with drugs to help us cope. This will only mask the problem. So then...***How do you cope?*** Coping is a learned behavior. Clearly understanding the issues you are faced with go much deeper than just the knowledge of knowing. You must be able to break things down. Once you can understand the circumstances that you are faced with, you can learn to navigate through any challenge. Sometimes taking a step back, finding a moment of stillness with breath work helps. Meditation can lead you out of the most stressful circumstances. You may also engage in physical exercise, which you may think is the complete opposite of meditation, when in fact they can be quite similar for your "mind". Both take your thoughts to "time out". You can also talk it out…express yourself. Sometimes having someone who will listen to you; someone you can express and share your feelings with, helps you to sort things through…invite it in!

Open the door to your mind. It's called **"Classic Thinking."** It teaches you to move through life, seeking awareness and ascending towards your needs. You will learn to cope. You will know that in time, these feelings held inside your mind will pass and that you will become stronger every day. You can live a happier and healthier life by learning to cope.

Ponder — I see clearly that I can cope with life
challenges that I may be confronted with —
What internal tools can I use to help clear my mind,
so I am able to cope?
How can I incorporate physical exercise
or mental meditation to quiet my mind?
How can I get creative so I can turn on my
"Classic Thinking?"

"Sometimes you need to be alone with your thoughts —
Only then can you choose which ones
you want to enter your mind."

— Dr. Jill Lee —

Manage Your Emotions

At the start of each new day; we have the opportunity to make new choices. The first choice we make is about our mindset or our mood. It's all about how you manage your emotions. Emotions are feelings that come from inside your heart space, and you may not even realize that you have options or choices, but you do.

What is your mood like the first thing in the morning? Do you wake up happy or sad? Are you feeling anxious? Are you looking forward to the day? Are there challenges ahead? These are all things that can be going through your mind first thing in the morning. How you answer these questions can set your mood for the entire day.

We all have times when we experience an array of emotions, without understanding what's behind them. You may think that there's no reason at all. Ah… but there is a reason. It's very common to feel this way without understanding, but the key is to get to the root and understand what's causing this world wind of raw and unprocessed emotions, and then releasing them. Perhaps a good cry will help. Yes — a good cry — because tears help wash away the pain of unspoken words, or suppressed emotions.

You can try to cover up or detach yourself from these wondrous feelings, by pretending they don't exist, or you can seek the driving force. If kept buried and unidentified, you may have the tendency to pass them on to others, unconsciously, therefore creating or causing others distress. It's the same as passing on a virus.

Behind your anger or sadness, there may be wounds that need to be healed, or there may be an unidentified fear. These locked emotions diminish any chances of joy in your life, if not addressed and managed. Once identified, you own them, and now you can face them head on. You can create your own authentic emotional release, that which works best for you.

You are in control. Each new day brings new choices. You can learn to rethink the beginning of each new day. Let love — kindness — empathy — and compassion lighten your heart and bring you — internal peace. A light heart is a happy heart — and so it goes.

Ponder *— I see clearly that I can manage my emotions —*
Do I have emotions that have not been addressed?
How can I release yet own my emotions?
What's behind and beneath these raw
or unidentified emotions?

"There's a simple pleasure in remembering —
There's a simple pleasure in wondering —
There's a simple pleasure in knowing —
If you are quiet enough — you can hear
your heart speak — for the heart always remembers."

— Dr. Jill Lee —

Every Choice Has A Consequence

We are all presented with choices from the moment we open our eyes in the morning. What to eat for breakfast? Coffee or tea? What to wear? These are simple everyday choices for most of us, but they are still choices. In reality, while it is important to make good choices; it's more about owning the choices you make. It's about taking responsibility or your actions. Life most often offers us the opportunity to decide what's right for us in the present moment. Too often, though; when making decisions, you aren't thinking about what consequences may follow. Your decisions are not always based on thoughtful contemplations. Some decisions are made on a whim or thoughtless impulse. Once you choose your action, the consequences that follow from your choice have a *will of their own.*

Before taking action, you may want to take a moment to analyze the situation, rather than make a hasty choice. Regardless of the circumstance, there are things to take into consideration. "How will my choices affect another person?" "How will my choices affect my position or well-being?" By asking such questions of yourself, before making an impulsive decision, you can often avoid unnecessary consequences.

You may not always make the perfect choices in your life, but if you think first; before charging forward… before you act, there's a better chance that things will turn out better than anticipated, not only for you but others involved. Look at the objectives, by weighing all the pros and cons. Remember that with every choice, comes a consequence, so choose wisely. Make sure the choices you make are "your" choices and not someone else's. Follow your instincts, but don't allow them to be in control. Learn to pause…then decide.

***Ponder** — I see clearly that my choices have consequences —*
Can I look at my choices objectively?
Am I able to follow through with the choices I make?
Will the choices I make serve my well-being?

"Find the time for that which touches your heart —
then choose."

— DR. JILL LEE —

Inner-Strength and Self-Discipline Your Power Within

Life can often be difficult when we are faced with obstacles and challenges. And it's how you navigate around each obstacle and overcome each challenge that will require self-discipline and inner strength. It's about your perception, interpretation, and attitude - good or bad - that will often dictate the outcome.

Inner-strength and self-discipline… it's about knowing who you are, not about aggression. It's about having moral and intellectual power, and using that power to follow through, and do what must be done, even during the most difficult times. It's about having the courage to feel your feelings, opening your heart and mind, and listening to your inner guidance.

You can generate or ignite this power when you take a "pause" before acting or reacting to a situation. When we were children, we were taught to "stop, look and listen" before crossing the street. The same principle can apply to any life situation. And when you understand the emotions that may be festering, you will realize that these emotions are an internal gift. It's the ability to "tap in" and be in charge of your life and the choices you make, those that best serve your well-being.

This gift may not be seen in a physical form, and often difficult to find, especially after experiencing a challenging time. But don't lose site and when you seem to be losing stamina…focus; it's there; you just need to see beyond the obvious.

Challenges are human experiences, and obstacles are just deterrents. Take all that's good in your life, and absorb it. Let it activate the positive side of your being, allowing you to develop happiness and peace within. Test and exercise your patience, determination, persistence and commitments. Identify and channel your thoughts as you tap into your inner strength. If you seem to be losing stamina...focus; it's there, this is where you will strengthen your self-discipline. Take responsibility and be accountable for your actions and reactions. Your positive attitude will help cultivate an optimistic point of view to the challenges you may face each day. And how you perceive each of these challenges will determine the quality of your life.

Ponder — *I see clearly that my attitude will affect*
the outcome of any given situation —
How can I take responsibility for my actions and reactions?
How can I test and exercise
my determination and persistence?
How can I strengthen my self-discipline
so I can navigate around any obstacles?

"Be brave, be strong, be confident. Listen to you inner
voice, the voice that speaks inside, the voice that whispers."

— DR. JILL LEE —

Release
Negative Emotions

Repressed or suppressed emotions can distort and alter the perception of your entire being; both psychological and physical. Containment of unexpressed emotions is a mode of communication; and an energy that will not go away or dissolve on its own, but will continue to accumulate within, causing tension, anxiety and frustration, not to mention the attacks on your physical body. Unhappiness and negativity is like a disease to the soul.

You might assume that a good cry or a demonstration of anger is a release, but that's only the beginning. Unless you reach the core of your emotions, they will continue to fester inside, creating anhedonia, stifling self-growth and healing.

A Five-step exercise to help you release

- Find the time and a quiet place to tap into your inner self. Locate the source of any negative patterns that may be bringing about these emotional toxins. Use your inner resources to become aware of your emotional climate, expanding your awareness.

- Identify and label each emotion. Is it fear, shame, regret, self-pity, resentment or anger? Whatever it is, give it a name…Express it and say it out loud.

- As you label your emotions, sit with it for a moment and feel it. Yes…feel the feeling.

- When you feel the emotion, ask yourself… "What lesson has it brought me?" Take responsibility and own it.

- Now it's time to release it — let it go.

You can release emotional energy in many different ways. Some people assign it to a star in the Universe. Some light a candle, exhale and send it up in smoke. You can also write it on paper, read it and then burn or shred the paper. Create a personal ritual; that which works best for you; there is no right or wrong way. *It's your way.* Do this as many times as needed. It can be challenging at times, but it is very necessary.

And most important, use the gentleness of your heart to help soothe, calm and heal. Realize that this emotional baggage needs to be released so you can enjoy your life being well-balanced, grounded and centered.

With courage and resilience, feel all of your feelings. Allow any emotions to flow *"through"* you, so that you can receive the message.

***Ponder** — I see clearly that I must release
suppressed or repressed emotions —
I can give a name or label to any negative emotion?
What type of ritual can I create to release my emotions?
What have I learned from this negative emotion,
now that it has been exposed?*

*"Oh — there is such power in our festering emotions —
Life has a way of helping us move through them —
When we are open to the current of life —
Trust the law and power of gravity —
allow your emotions to flow."*

— DR. JILL LEE —

Change Promotes Growth

So very often, we as humans resistant change. Change can sometimes bring uncertainty and unpredictability. It moves us away from what's familiar and very often comfortable. If you generate and maintain an air of optimism, you will communicate change and growth. When you understand that change leads to growth and growth leads to change, you realize the essence of the life your living. This is an internal process which requires self-inquiry and allows both change and growth to take place. Only when you understand this concept, can you dissolve any fears that may be getting in your way. It also requires self- understanding, self-respect, and self-responsibility to recognize your strengths and weaknesses, so you can move through any uncertainties and accept any challenges you may not be ready to face.

Each shift you encounter brings about new beginnings, new experiences, and new opportunities. You may also be presented with new challenges. However, this can only stimulate personal growth. Sometimes it may require that you step outside your comfort zone and move away from your redundant routine. When you do the same thing day after day, over and over again, life becomes stagnant. Things don't change. Be reminded that growth is part of life — change is an option.

There will be times that require you to give something up, to make change happen, and you may find that you are bargaining with yourself. Asking… *"What am I willing to give up for growth and change? How difficult can it be? What do I have to gain?"* When you stop and ponder some, and ask these questions of yourself, you may be very pleasantly surprised with your answers. As you take responsibility for your decisions, you are creating self-discipline. You are holding yourself accountable. Only then are you able to make the necessary choices to bring about change.

Learn to embrace diversity, and you will overcome any obstacles that may be in your path. Learn to breathe in the crisp air, and enjoy the shift, the same way you enjoy the changing of seasons. Let your ambitions be the food for your desire, and fill any emptiness you may have in your soul.

Ponder — *I see clearly that I must shift out of my comfort
zone to enjoy the possibilities of change
and personal growth —
What obstacles are holding me back
from stepping out of my comfort zone?
How difficult can change be?
How can I embrace diversity?*

*"Cultivate your mind. Know that change
promotes growth and change requires change
— your time is now."*

— Dr. Jill Lee —

Expand Your Personal Boundaries

All through our life, we tend to cling to what's familiar and comfortable, not wanting to accept change. When change occurs, we might feel a sense of loss; exposing emotions of sadness or anxiety, and even frustration. These are all natural reactions. And where do these feelings come from? Most often fear. Fear is one thing that can hold you back from making changes in your life. Sometimes the nature of feeling comfort or familiarity can lead to delusions or mislead you down the wrong path. You are then lost or stuck in a place "where you are" instead of "where you are meant to be", or "where you want to be."

Learning to expand your thinking mind is where the change begins. Listening, that comes from a deeper place than from your ears. That means stretching your personal boundaries and not living complacent or living in a controlled compartment. There is no need to punish yourself by staying where you don't belong, or where you don't want to be. There are lingering benefits in life by giving yourself permission to step out of your comfort zone. Your mind will need to travel — before you arrive.

Like any other changes in life, stepping out of your comfort zone is a learned behavior. Start slow, and set conscious intentions. Know what inspires you and go for it one step at a time. The further you step outside your comfort zone the easier in time it becomes, leading you to new and exciting experiences. It can guide you to new beginnings, taking you in new directions, and challenging you to learn new things.

Be committed to your own path and trust your inner self. "Is it right for me?" That's what really matters most. Remember that when you love where you are in life, you gain contentment. Allow change to happen, but make sure you find your balance with comfort.

Ponder — *I see clearly that I can I am in control
of allowing "change" in my life —
Is familiarity and comfort holding me back
from making changes?
How can I face my fear of change?
How can I stretch my personal boundaries?*

*"Find inner peace with your journey —
wherever it may lead you —
It allows you the freedom to be who you are.
Let your heart and soul guide you."*

— DR. JILL LEE —

WEEK THIRTEEN

Knowing Your True Self

I am sure at one time or another you have asked yourself "Who am I?" Discovering who you really are is a lifetime mission. That's because we are forever changing and recognizing something new about ourselves. Discovery comes from our own life experiences. Each of us has our own unique identity.

Discovering oneself is self-awareness. Knowing your values and holding true to them says a lot about your authentic self. It's your character and your integrity that defines you. It's not about the clothes you wear, or who you socialize with. It's not about how much money you have or have not. It's about who you are on the inside.

Self-awareness means paying attention to what's inside your soul; going back to your core values. When you know who you are, you create an intention that will broaden your mind to body connection. This connection will help you develop self-empowerment, allowing you to make wiser choices in life.

Every choice you make in life, leads to who you are and the life you are living. Wise choices can make you a better person while other choices can be destructive. Knowing the difference and making the necessary changes is where the self-awareness comes in. What do you attach yourself to? How do you allow yourself to "feel"? Taking responsibility for yourself lets you define and refine your identity. You can restore anything damaged or hurt by knowing the answers to these questions.

Align yourself with the inner "you". Know what motivates you and what you are most passionate about. Knowing and liking yourself generates self-worth and promotes strong self-esteem. Every day, invite these beautiful visions of yourself into your life. You must hold these visions of who you are, to make the necessary changes. Let go of what no longer serves your well-being, so there is space for new growth.

Remember that everything in this life leads you to the life you are living or the life you choose to live.

Ponder *— I see clearly that I have a unique identity, and I*
like what I see —
What motivates me?
Do my choices define me?
Do my choices serve my well-being?

"Self-empowerment allows you to know
your strengths and weaknesses.
You must know your "self"
to understand who and what you are."

— DR. JILL LEE —

Doubt Your Doubts

Even the most confident people get a visit from "Self-Doubt." This visitor; and I use the term "visitor" because it is not a permanent condition or state of being; can cause you to second guess yourself. It's a temporary lack of self-confidence. It brings about fear, resistance, and even procrastination. When you find yourself being pulled by negative or doubtful thoughts, recognize that it's simply a message for you to pay attention to your inner voice; and perhaps a reminder to follow your intuition. Remember that doubt doesn't always mean don't. Identify the doubt, and don't over analyze it or get lost in it.

You may want to take a "time out" during these moments of uncertainties. Pause for just a few moments and find stillness. Create a vision within your mind…of the results…of the direction or path you're moving towards. See it…and then feel it. *What is your intuition telling you to do?* This is where you can doubt your doubts and begin to believe in yourself. Become aware and know the "why"; then listen and follow that voice inside.

Nothing can destroy your creativity and dreams quicker than "self-doubt". When you learn to trust your values, you become confident, and won't be discouraged from achieving your set goals or dreams. You take action, and you get out of your own way, moving towards a path that feels right for you. Stay committed with self-confidence and without excuses. Raise your awareness and become conscious and *never* underestimate the power and relevancy of "self-doubt." Don't harbor it, as doubt can sabotage and destroy your beliefs as well as your intentions. Doubt the doubt and let your determination help you move through any challenges, to meet your quest.

> ***Ponder*** *— I see clearly that my doubts are just doubts —*
> *How can I raise my awareness and become more*
> *conscious to discard these doubts?*
> *Can I hear my inner voice guiding me?*
> *Can I allow my determination and perseverance*
> *take over my doubts?*

> *"Don't allow weeds to grow inside your soul*
> *and cover the light that shines within —*
> *Capture your light — and let it shine —*
> *so you can grow and blossom."*
>
> — DR. JILL LEE —

Are You Settling?

Do you ever have the feeling that something may be missing in your life? Are you settling for less than you deserve or desire? So often we become complacent and settle for oddments of pleasures because we may be afraid to look or go beyond our fear based thoughts. Thoughts that create doubt or resistance. However, when you address these thoughts and see them for what they truly are, you realize that you have complete control to modify and move beyond this narrowed thinking. You realize that you have choices.

Whether it's in your personal or professional life, it all applies. It's easy to make excuses why you "can't" do something, have something, or change something. Let's list a few and see if they sound familiar:

- I'm not good enough

- Doubting self-worth

- Fear of change

- It's easier to stay

- I don't have time

- I feel bad for him/her

- I'm not ready

- It's too hard

- I'm too old

- It's already been done

These are just a few, as there is an endless list of excuses that one can make, not to move forward and live your best life. You must confront these excuses when they come into your thoughts, instead of allowing them to hold you back. Take each one of this listed excuses and turn it around. There is a positive for every negative!

Where is your passion? What motivates you? What's calling you? Only you have the answers. Quiet your mind, and listen. Remember, though, there are no shortcuts, you have to do the work, and that's not to say that it will always be easy.

Make a bold commitment to act and not procrastinate. Make the commitment to change. Make the commitment to grow. Your destiny is all within reach, and you hold the power to make it all happen. It's your passion and intense desires that create limitless opportunities. You are the vessel; allow your passions and desires to enter.

Ponder *— I see clearly that I do not have to "just settle"*
as life offers me limitless opportunities —
Are there areas in my life where I have become complacent?
Can I modify each excuse and change
it to a positive choice?
How can I move beyond the resistance for change?

"You deserve a full life — a life filled with more
than oddments of pleasure.
It's there — and it's yours for the taking."

— DR. JILL LEE —

WEEK SIXTEEN

Living With Integrity

Integrity is when your thoughts, your words, and your actions are all aligned. It's also about doing the right thing, even when no one is watching. It's when you live and behave congruently with strong core values. It's a quality that comes from the inside, yet shines on the outside. When you live with integrity, you never have to second-guess your intentions. Your values and ethics guide you.

Staying true to your values, morals, and ethical principles, is the key to being your authentic self with sound and moral character. And the good thing about that is that no one can ever take that away from you. It's personal, it's yours, and you own it! It's a state of being whole, entire, and undiminished, regardless of what others may think.

Sometimes in life, we're confronted with choices or decisions that may seem difficult. Don't hold back, stay true to yourself. With dignity and integrity, never compromise your self-respect. The important thing to remember is always to stand up for what you believe. Know what's meaningful to you, in your heart of hearts, and let that lead your mind.

Let your integrity preserve who you are. Reach into your emotional intelligence and acknowledge your true feelings, without judgment. Be honest with yourself. You build your reputation with integrity, by not compromising your core principles for anyone, at any time.

Living with integrity allows you to live life as your best self. Carry this state of being with you always, both in your personal and professional life. You will maintain an excellent sense of self-respect while earning the respect of others. Integrity is a virtue that you should continue to strive for, all the days of your life. Having integrity is one of the most significant characteristics any human can possess. It's your greatest asset.

***Ponder** — I see clearly that I must*
stay true to my core values —
Am I honest with myself — about my core principles?
How can I maintain my dignity,
while earning the respect of others?
Do my life- choices affect my integrity?

"Having integrity is one of the most
significant characteristics any human can possess.
It's your greatest asset."

— DR. JILL LEE —

Creative Mind Energy

There is creative energy in your mind that can help you break out of mundane thinking habits in your life; as you know it. As humans, we all have this prodigious energy within our minds, so often untapped. It's there, however; the energy lies dormant, as we are so often consumed with everyday rituals and activities. We meet our daily challenges and most often move through them with the knowledge we have first-hand. But what happens when you go beyond your immediate thoughts? What happens when you think outside the box?

We seem to be comfortable with our general thinking patterns because that's how we've been taught, and it's by repetition or habit, we resolve most conflicts.

When your mind is on overload, and you are multitasking; when you are consumed with a heavy workload and no time to "think", you limit or deplete your creative mind energy. You'll find yourself reacting to situations, rather than responding to them, or making hasty decisions, simply due to the lack of time; compromising the outcome.

When you center your thoughts, you are able to move through your day with clear and focused intentions. Slow down, reflect, and see things beyond as they are and begin to use your creative mind energy. It helps you break those stagnate behavior patterns of thought. You then stimulate and ignite movement in your mind, noticing an abundance of possibilities and defining your expression. You don't need to limit yourself to what you already know. By changing the flow of energy, you cultivate and expand your mind.

Don't underestimate the power of "thought". Watch, as your creative energy stimulates and ignites your mind movement and maximizes your potential. Creative mind energy can propel you to places you never anticipated…and beyond.

***Ponder** — I see clearly that thinking beyond
the obvious can change everyday habits —
How can I tap into my creative mind energy?
Can my thoughts have a direct effect on the choices I make?
What can ignite my thoughts, so I start thinking
"outside the box?"*

*"Don't underestimate the power of those
emotional events in your life —
Creative mind energy helps you think with passion;
beyond the obvious —
It's your creative stimulation that ignites mind-movement."*

— DR. JILL LEE —

Imperfection or Unique?

"Imperfection" What is it? Most of us would say that is someone or something that has flaws, defects, or perhaps faults. Someone or something that is less than perfect. But by whose standards are these imperfections defined? *Steve Maraboli describes it best. "Imperfections are illusions caused by expectation. They are a psychological warning that we are not seeing true potential, but self- imposed limitation".*

We all have imperfections, but it's how we perceive them, what we do with them and how we value ourselves that helps create who we are in life. When you look at your imperfections and accept them as part of who you are, they can become your most attractive characteristics. (As long as it brings no harm to others). Each distinctive trait you have shouldn't be defined as right or wrong, but more about how it defines who you are. One person's imperfection is another person's uniqueness.

When you get past your ego based thoughts and be who you dare to be; it may expose your vulnerability and show you that your imperfections are part of being human. See them for what they are, and grow with them. Let others love you because of your imperfections, not in spite of them. Let go of who you think you should be, and embrace all that you are.

You are the owner of your imperfections and uniqueness. The choices you make create the structure of your life and should empower you. The more you accept your individuality, the easier it becomes to live your life with your so-called "imperfections." Being perfectly imperfect is okay.

Share your beautiful humanness with the world. It means that you shouldn't take yourself too seriously, because things happen in life, regardless of how much structure there may be. It means not limiting yourself to what others may think or what their expectations are of you.

Be in harmony with all that you are and look beyond your imperfections.

Ponder *— I see clearly that my
imperfections are part of what makes me unique —
How can I create a harmony between my
imperfections and my uniqueness?
Can I move past my thoughts of what I think others…
think I should be?
Can I see the "beautiful me," beyond my imperfections?*

*"It's your imperfections that make you perfect —
and your flaws that make you flawless —
It's who you are."*

— Dr. Jill Lee —

Live With Intent

Intent - "Determined to do something." What a fabulous way to live. Do you know who you are and what you want out of life? When you live your life with intention, you create and manifest your reality. Living with intent is a state of being, and it creates purpose. It's a form of "being" that helps you to create the action.

So you may ask where does this "intention" come from or how do I get it? You start by calming yourself and finding your center. You listen to your inner voice and trust what you hear. Trust what you know to be true. Once you have defined your intention or intentions, you take ownership. It's yours and yours alone. Can you see it? Now decide how this will connect with other elements in your life. Visualize how it will enrich your life. Let go of any negative thoughts that may hold you back from taking action. Let your energy flow where your attention goes. This attention is called living deliberately and with purpose. It's your personal aspirations that can shape your life and create your destiny.

Creating an intention and letting it guide you, helps in many areas of your life. It encourages creativity and allows you to have visionary control over your life…with direction. As you integrate intent into your daily life, you begin to feel satisfied and fulfilled. Take the time to explore different opportunities.

Be gentle with yourself. This process takes discipline and commitment. Life is made up of a series of choices. Your choices. Know your values, your strengths, and your passions. Let go of expectations and be open to change. Be mindful, yet curious. Develop content for your life, and commit. It's your life to live. Why waste precious days away stumbling through, or wandering aimlessly? Know what inspires you.

Don't just exist. Make it part of your daily routine, to start each day with a deliberate intention. Don't surrender to limitations. Your visions, your success, and your happiness is all within your intent.

> ***Ponder*** — *I see clearly that each choice I make*
> *must be deliberate and with intention —*
> *How do I take ownership of my choices?*
> *Do I know my strengths and passions?*
> *How do I not allow myself to surrender to limitations?*

"Live each day with intent — deliberately — and on purpose."

— Dr. Jill Lee —

Unclutter Your Life

Do you feel that your world can use some decluttering? I think that is something we all can honestly admit to. Our home, our workspace, and even our calendars. I use the word "we" because I am right there with you! You can simplify your life; physically, emotionally, and mentally, by lightening your load, organizing, and prioritizing. Giving yourself free space, a path for clarity.

When there is a lot of clutter, it's easy to become overwhelmed and frustrated when needing to find something and you have to sort through piles or rummage through drawers to find it. *I know it's here…but where?* What a waste of time and effort, not to mention what it does to your emotional state of being.

Do you have so much "stuff" and nowhere to put it all? Do you have piles of "stuff" and have difficulty when needing to find something?

Do you have too many commitments on your calendar and not enough free time? Well if the answer is "yes" to any one of these questions, then it's time to unclutter your world!

Starting with your home, here are a few suggestions to help you start the process:

- Start systematically with small tasks. Look around each room and see if there are things that really don't have significant importance to you. Ask yourself... *"Do I really need this?"* That's when you start to create space.

- Begin with one shelf or countertop in each room at a time. Perhaps there are things that you are now ready to part with. Maybe you can gift them on to a family member so they can enjoy these treasures, as you did over the years. Maybe donate to charity, those things that you are not using. Make sure that whatever you decide to *keep*; has its own place so you can see it and enjoy it. Remember that this is a process, and it's going to take some time. Don't overwhelm yourself by trying to do too much at once.

- Try to set aside 30 minutes a day to declutter, and then return the next day...The same goes for any piles you may have to go through, or closets and drawers that need to be cleaned out, until you have gone through each room. Just keep chipping away, a little each day. Before you know it, you will look around and enjoy the organized space you have created for yourself.

- What about your workspace? How do you feel when you get to work? Are you overwhelmed or stressed when you look at your desk? Do you have piles that need to be filed? You may say *"I know where everything is"* but the fact is when you need something quickly, you still have to sort through those piles.

- You might start by setting an appointment for each pile, based on priorities. Create folders and label them so you know where everything is at a glance. Don't create additional piles and don't put anything back into those existing piles. Learn to file quickly. You will be much more productive and work more efficiently when working in an organized workspace.

- How's your personal calendar? You can reduce your commitments by learning to say no to non-essential things. Create your to-do list and organize your priorities, then declutter the rest. There is no need to overload yourself. Find your balance. Your time is valuable, and you deserve to enjoy your "free time".

We all have clutter that can be eliminated or at the least; reduced. When you begin to lighten your load, simplify and organize; you create mental space for yourself. You also establish a more peaceful environment for your home life and your workplace.

Ponder — I see clearly that an organized space
creates a peaceful environment.
How much time can I set aside each day to
declutter my home or work space?
Do I have "stuff" that I no longer need and can dispose of?
Can I reduce any commitments, so I have more "me" time?

"Life feels peaceful with less clutter,
it gives me 'breathing and thinking mind space."

— Dr. Jill Lee —

WEEK TWENTY-ONE

Your Character

What is it that makes up your individual character? It 's the combination of your values, your thoughts, and how you speak to others, as well as your actions, and ethical traits — your integrity. Your character says more about you and is more important than your reputation, because again, your character is who you are, whereas your reputation is what others think you are. So with this in mind, *what does your character say about you? Are you the person you would like to be?*

Take time to explore; go deep within and ask questions of yourself. Am I kind and empathetic? Do I have humility? These are questions that only you can answer.

Each experience you encounter, each choice you make in life, helps you to develop your character. How your respond to situations and circumstances, defines your character. It's not about your financial status; it's about your core values, your integrity as well as your behavior. How you treat others says a lot about who you are. How you make others feel when they are in your presence, also speaks volumes about who you are.

How would you like to be defined or remembered? What do you want others to take away after you've had a brief conversation? Again, only you can answer these questions, and they are all important.

Keep in mind that to have good character is to have strong, moral values and beliefs. It's one who shows compassion and maintains integrity, when no one is watching — and when everyone is watching. Your character — your integrity — belongs to you. No one can ever take it away.

Ponder — I see clearly that my values, my choices
and my actions make up my character —
Am I kind and empathetic?
Can the way I respond to situations and
circumstances change my character?
Am I the kind of person I would like to be?

"Watch your thoughts, they become words; watch your
words, they become actions; watch your actions, they
become habits; watch your habits, they become character;
watch your character, for it becomes your destiny."

— Frank Outlaw —

Your Core Beliefs

Belief is a mental representation or expression of your personal opinion. And it's by these beliefs that influence the way we live our lives. They can lead you to the choices you make both in your personal and professional life. How are these beliefs formed? Sometimes they are cultural, or religious based. Some were instilled in you by your elders or just acquired at a very early age. And then there are those beliefs that you've created in your mind, based on your own illusions or thoughts of how you *think* things should be. But none are written in stone. Each of your beliefs can be maintained, modified or relinquished at any time.

Regardless of where your beliefs come from, they belong to you. Are you able to identify them? *Do your beliefs control you or do you control your beliefs?* They can be the inspirational force that leads you to incredible possibilities and opportunities in your life. The

Encyclopedia Britannica, Inc. states; *"belief is arguably the most powerful and potent force in human behavior."*

By identifying, understanding and evaluating the nature of your core beliefs, you can facilitate change in your life's patterns and choices. Many of your beliefs may be bundled together, and you may not be able to change them until you start breaking them apart. You can then decide whether they are assumptions or facts of life. Each may not necessarily need a reason behind them; they may just be your perception. It's all about how *you* define each belief.

The manifestation of your beliefs is who you are. They affect all that you do, the choices you make, as well as your relationships with others. They have the power to pull you back, or they can be like a magnet drawing you to fantastic opportunities, creating a new reality.

The key to dissecting and understanding; is to rethink and go beyond your thoughts. You decide if your beliefs best serve your well-being or if they are holding you back from living the life you aspire to live. Let your core beliefs be the magnet for exciting, new opportunities.

Remember that belief precedes knowledge. Be mindful and don't ignore any facts that may bring light to your existing or new ideas. It just may lead to a change in your perception of life as your know it.

***Ponder** — I see clearly that my beliefs
are a reflection of who I am —
Where do my strongest beliefs come from,
and are they true "my personal beliefs."
Do my beliefs control or hold me back
from life's opportunities?
Can I modify my beliefs without changing my core values?*

*"Your core beliefs is who you are —
or is who you are your core beliefs?
Are they one of the same?"*

— DR. JILL LEE —

WEEK TWENTY-THREE

Resolving Conflicts

onflicts can be triggered at most any time and for the most trivial reasons. Unfortunately, we can't always choose the time or the place they arrive. Conflicts can happen in the workplace or at home, and with family, friends or with any personal relationship.

Many conflicts arise from differences of opinions, different thought processes, or different values. Sometimes conflicts arise from misunderstandings. Conflicts can arise when there is tension in a situation, or when issues need to be addressed and discussed, issues that have perhaps…have been silenced.

So where do you begin? You should always try to clarify the conflict, rather than form an assumption. This will help you find a healthy balance when communicating. Respect, consideration and empathy;

of all parties involved play a significant role in the success of find-ing a resolution. A respectful discussion may bring about thoughts, feelings and opinions that are perhaps hidden. Sometimes, what you are most passionate about might need to be exposed and expressed, even though these emotions may lead to hurt feelings. It brings forth clarity.

As conflicts emerge, recognize them as just that. A conflict; and that's just part of life, many times unavoidable, no matter how we try. Most personal conflicts can be resolved, but it starts with emotional awareness and mindful communication. There may be sensitive situ-ations that cause an argument or even silence. There may be a hidden agenda that needs to be uncovered and dealt with. Be mindful and realize that we all have the need to be heard and understood. Try to see beyond the layers of debris. You may find a hidden treasure there, a blessing in disguise.

When resolving conflicts, it's important to listen beyond the spoken words. Choose your battles wisely; it's not always about who's right or wrong. Know when to let things go, or when to walk away, and most importantly, be willing to forgive.

Ponder — *I see clearly that I must be open to resolving*
a conflict as there are two sides to each story —
Can I hear the unspoken words in a conversation?
How can I see and think beyond the layers of debris?
Am I able to respect others,
even if they don't share my opinions?

"You must learn to move through,
and grow from each conflict
Treat each conflict as a gift,
as it teaches and enables you to transform your life."

— Dr. Jill Lee

WEEK TWENTY-FOUR

Words Matter

The sound that presses through your lips called "words" carries such power. Your words spoken are more than just elements of speech; they are living expressions of basic vibrations, coming from your voice box that transmits a powerful energy force. Those words are consumed and absorbed by others. They can have a lingering effect, are not easily forgotten. You've all heard the phrase "Think before you speak." Your words matter and more than you may realize.

Words are a deliberate act of sound, although not always coming from a conscious place or thought, and once spoken, they cannot be retracted. There are times when one is so overwhelmed or absorbed with "self"; that they may be unaware of the impact their words have on others and the true messages they carry. You have the ability to change an entire relationship in a matter of moments; by simply being mindful of the words you speak, and how you speak them.

Soft words imply and deliver gentleness and kindness while harsh words generate anger and bitterness. Your words can soothe and comfort, or destroy and harm. They can be humiliating or humbling, healing or hindering. Your words have the power to enter the hearts and minds of others. It's often been said that "the mouth is an entrance to the heart, as well as the exit."

When communicating with others, always speak with mindfulness and show compassion. Speak with simplicity and ease. Speak from your heart, and allow your words to flow effortlessly, with a tone that others will want to hear. Know that there is as much importance to what you say, as to how you say it. Let your words, and how you communicate with others, be part of your character. It's one of the most powerful forces of humanity.

Remember that your words will live in the hearts and minds others, for a very long time. Your voice is the gateway to your inner and outer self, and can say a lot about who you are.

Ponder — *I see clearly that my spoken words are absorbed*
and consumed by others. I must be mindful
when communicating with others —
How can I become more selective in the words
I use to express myself to others?
Can I soften a spoken phrase,
so that my words are better understood?
Does the tone of how I speak, reflect what I speak?

"Be mindful to use your words in a way that
delivers kindness — Let others feel your words
in a soft and compassionate way.
Don't allow harsh or hurtful words —
pass through your lips."

— Dr. Jill Lee —

Dealing With Disappointment

Often, one may be confronted with disappointments. You may even feel that there are times that the odds are stacked against you. These frustrations create internal emotions and are sometimes difficult for us to understand or manage. These emotions may even narrow your point of perception of any given situation.

Perhaps there is an unforeseen reason for what's happened or why things didn't go your way. With this being said, you cannot allow it to destroy your desires or ambitions. Although you may see it as monumental, don't view it as personal, as it touches all of us at some point in our lives. Don't lose hope and don't give up. Express the hurt; cry if you must, then look for solutions or compromises that serve you best. Modify your mindset and make the necessary adjustment to your thoughts and expectations. This is an opportunity to tap into your consciousness. You now have the chance to take this experience and give it meaning and purpose.

Let your desires drive and motivate you, not your expectations. Release your mental illusions and disempower the negative energy. Practice acceptance, as these experiences are part of life. Take time to see the big picture, perhaps in a different light.

And most important, don't allow yourself to dwell…try again. A new path may bring a new outcome. See the situation as an opportunity for growth, and use the lesson to help you surge forward, taking you in a new direction to reach your desired goals.

How you perceive and deal with each situation, can determine the quality of your life. Remember your core values and trust your heart. There is a message that comes along with each disappointment. It only means that there is something better on the horizon, and this is all part of your life's journey. Stand tall and keep moving forward. The Universe intends for you to do so. Believe in yourself, and you can defy all odds.

Ponder — *I see clearly that there is a reason and a lesson
given for each unexpected disappointment I encounter —
Can I see beyond my disappointments?
How can I shed light and change direction on
a situation that has not gone my way?
Can I express my hurt and frustration out loud,
and then move forward?*

*"There are unforeseen reasons for what's happened
from these unexpected circumstances or expectations.
It's part of your life's journey."*

— DR. JILL LEE —

Rise Above Adversity

The word adversity is a noun that has so many meanings and interpretations; different for everyone. It relates to misfortune, difficulty, or tribulation. It also can mean disaster or suffering, even grief; just to mention a few. There is no way to measure the magnitude or intensity of adversity as it comes to each and every one of us sometime during our life here on earth. Know that sometimes bad things happen to good people. It's part of life.

Situations happen to us, and don't always happen for the best, but they do happen for a reason. It's been said that *"there are times when things must go wrong so that they can go right."* And although the reason may not be apparent right away, be aware and alert. You must give yourself permission to be human; as you acknowledge and accept what has comes your way. It's your courage and strength that will help you to endure each struggle or challenge. And it's with your internal resources that you learn to rise above it all.

Although adversity brings about fear and anxiety, not to mention many other emotions; it's determination, resilience, and persistence that will help you most through these difficult times. You must, however; not allow these negative feelings of despair to take over and empower your mind. Look beyond each situation and ask yourself… "How can I make it better?" Choose to choose, and focus on what you "can" do.

Each adversity; while it may challenge you; is a life lesson. Each situation that you are confronted with will build character, and make you wiser and stronger than ever before. It will help to shape who you are as a person. Accept this change as it comes about, because through adversity comes greatness.

Your inner strength, grace, and wisdom, will help you maintain your dignity and integrity through each adversity, by doing the right thing and making the right choices. Have faith that in time, the pain or hurt will fade. Have the wisdom to know the lessons will remain forever.

Ponder — *I see clearly that I can choose to rise
above adversity with grace and wisdom —
How can I move beyond my fear of facing
a difficult situation?
Can I accept each challenge as it comes in my direction?
Can I choose to choose?*

*"When you confront adversity straight on —
you begin to realize there may be a blessing in disguise.
Use your internal resources to move through it."*

— DR. JILL LEE —

Your Peace, Your Serenity

Serenity" as defined in the dictionary is "the absence of mental stress or anxiety." It's the gateway to being in touch with your higher self. What a beautiful way to begin your day. Perhaps you can start a morning ritual; breakfast with morning with a dish of calm and gratitude…Ahhhh…a ritual of self-love.

The world we live in is loud and noisy. We are so often wrapped up by the all the challenges and daily tasks; we forget about how beautiful it is to bask in serenity, our personal sanctuary for peace; your Zen. It's essential to our existence that we have peace of mind in our lives. An internal place where there is calm and tranquility.

You may often hear me speak of *quieting the mind chatter* and that's because it is of such importance. This will allow you, in a moments time, to become aware of your surroundings and your environment, wherever you may be, to find a moment of stillness. This becomes your space; where you can bring attention to your being, a place where you can contemplate blessings. There are times where your mind may want to wander, so pay attention to where it goes and try not to allow it to wander off course. You can do this by anchoring your wandering thoughts with intent and allowing tranquility to come to you, through the consciousness of "self."

Know that this is not necessarily a physical space; but more of a mental space. This is a place where you can release negative thoughts and clear the way for positive intentions and choices. A place where you reset, and soften your words, allowing them to become kind and compassionate. A place where you find forgiveness, not only for others but also for yourself. These are the moments that will bring you sweet serenity.

Try to make time each day for beautiful moments of silence and stillness. This is where you will get to know the deepest part of your inner-self. You do this by clearing away any and all distractions, and then you engage yourself in the luxury of just being.

Question: When peace and serenity are absent, where do you feel it first?
Answer: First in your mind, then in your being.

Question: When peace and serenity become apparent, where do you feel it first?
Answer: In your heart.

Ponder — *I see clearly that I can create my own*
sanctuary of peace, serenity and Zen —
How can I quiet the chatter in my mind and find stillness?
What morning ritual can I create,
so that I can begin my day with calm?
How can I soften and anchor my thoughts so I can
create positive intentions, which will clear a path
to better choices?

"Peace and Serenity await you — It's in your mind —
your thoughts — your soul — and resides in your heart."

— DR. JILL LEE —

WEEK TWENTY-EIGHT

Needs vs. Desires

Needs are most often necessities in life. They are essential things that are easy to recognize, such as air, water, food and shelter; these are things necessary for survival.

Desire, on the other hand, is a natural yearning; an emotional impulse, and a hunger that moves you towards something greater. Desire is something that touches and nourishes the deepest part of your heart and soul.

The problem arises when you are not able to recognize the difference. Then the "need" for desire, distorts your perception. You become propelled by your emotions, which changes your psychological mindset. Your perception of "need" tends to grow with intensity, and then a fine line is created as well as attachments to things, like material wealth. Does that come from need or desire?

Ask yourself...*Are there needs in my desires? Are there desires in my needs?*

It is most important to create a balance. Know that it takes work, reflection and self-awareness to recognize the difference and obtain clarity. This is all part of personal development, and this does take time and attention. Understand that *desire* gently pulls and guides whereas *needs* can be driven from your egoic mind. Desire is soft and encouraging while needs can be loud and demanding.

While there are things in life that are a necessity, don't allow it to take over and change who you are. Don't allow it to become your desperations or obsessions. Yes, the heart is hungry, and the soul is thirsty. Let your desires be fuel for your creativity and passions. Let it ignite you, and move you. Let it become your aliveness.

Ponder — *I see clearly that there is a difference
between my needs and desires —
Have I allowed my desires to become a
source of desperation?
Are my needs things that I desire?
How can I create a balance with what I need…
so I can realize my desired passions?*

*"Plant your feelings — feel your emotions. Let them grow
and blossom. When the soul grows — The heart opens.
This is evidence of human seasons."*

— DR. JILL LEE —

Letting Go of Guilt

One of the most disruptive human emotions to live with is "guilt". It can be quite burdensome and cause you great distress. Guilt can also spur you to make poor life choices, and perhaps move you in a direction that works against your core beliefs, causing you to fight with your inner-self.

Guilt shows up for many different reasons and in many different ways. It can come from disappointments; which might be failures of your personal expectations. Perhaps there is a mistake you've made or a wrong-doing. Maybe you offended someone or misspoke.

Another type of guilt is "false guilt". It's guilt misplaced on you, by others. It's when someone tries to shame you into doing something against your free-will or your beliefs, for their personal gain. You may even have been blamed or punished for something another person thought was wrong. Regardless of where it comes from, guilt and shame can tie your insides into knots. It's an ugly emotion, a demon that lives within when allowed to fester.

Guilt is a form of non-forgiveness and promotes self-pity. Don't let your pride stand in the way of moving forward. You cannot undo the past. Yes, take responsibility. If you can right a wrong, then do so. If you can apologize, then do so. Know that you can only take responsibility for *your* actions. Don't become obsessed with this feeling of guilt and allow it to take over or control you. Set yourself free, for there is no need to continue punishing yourself. Staying true to what you believe is not being riotous; it's being of sound mind.

With this being said, you do not have to live with this ugly emotion, named "guilt" It can make matters appear to be worse than they are. When you know and understand where it's coming from, you then can grab hold of it, and turn it into self-growth and a lesson learned. You are human and humans make mistakes. Don't dwell on the "should have", what's done is done. Forgive yourself; then let it go and move on.

Your inner-self knows what's best for you...you just need to listen. Listen to what your "gut" tells you…And to what your "heart" tells you. Stay true to your core beliefs; what feels right for you and don't allow others to manipulate you, by trying to instill guilt in you. There is no amount of guilt worth disrupting your inner-peace.

***Ponder** — I see clearly that holding on to guilt
disrupts my inner-peace —
Can I take responsibility to right a wrong,
instead of holding on to ill-feelings?
Can I forgive myself for any wrong doings and
let go of the guilt I am harboring?
Am I able to stay true to my core beliefs, doing what I feel
is right, without allowing others to instill guilt in me?*

*"With the grace of your being,
forgive yourself and release your guilt.
Let it lead you to change that can be useful
in your day to day life."*

— DR. JILL LEE —

WEEK THIRTY

Ego

As described philosophically in the dictionary; *"ego is the part of the psychic apparatus that experiences and reacts to the outside world and thus mediates between the primitive drives of the id (that which resides in the unconscious) and the demands of the social and physical environment."*

And with that being said, ego is part of who we are; often part of "self-image." If not controlled, you become overpowered by "I", "Me" and "Mine". I am not sure that the ego can be entirely dismissed or dissolved, but it can definitely be tamed and redirected. This can often be challenging.

If not tamed, ego has the tendency to sabotage relationships, or stand in the way of proceeding with opportunities. It can also cloud your judgment, creating a false sense of fear; a false sense of reality. If you allow your ego to take over, your thoughts begin to circle. You find yourself needing validation, which is the lack of self-esteem. You may have the need to blame others when things go awry, and become unable to forgive. You become trapped in playing the victim, and unable to resolve conflicts, and this can build anxiety and bring about stress.

By becoming aware and being mindful of this "ego", you gain control. You let your spirit override and realign your true authentic self. Know who you are. You then soften, when confronted with harshness; you forgive when there is anger. You become selfless, giving and sharing; with grace and empathy, and without bias. You learn that it's not always about winning or the need to be right, and you let go of judgment. You embrace gratitude.

Listen to your internal voice and shift your awareness; let your spirit speak. This occurs when you are fully present. Consciousness will bring your life into balance, with harmony and peace.

***Ponder** — I see clearly that my "ego"
is indeed part of my "self-image" —
Am I able to recognize when my "ego" is present?
How can I tame or redirect my ego, so it does
not overpower and cloud my judgment?
Where can I soften and let go of resentments
so I can enjoy balance, harmony, and peace?*

*"Open your mind and don't be misguided by your "ego."
"Ego" can be the destroyer of relationships and
can be food for other people's hearts."*

— DR. JILL LEE

Circumstances Brings Opportunities

What exactly is an "opportunity" and where does it come from? Well — It's a set of circumstances, that can come to you at any given time, that make it possible for you to make changes in your life, changes that can help you grow. They come by way of chance, luck, or timing. It can come about through curiosity, courage, and even spontaneity. There is no need to label it or see it as an obstacle. Opportunities, when pursued, can lead or guide you to your destiny and self-greatness.

So often, opportunities come knocking on your door, sometimes disguised and easy to miss. Perhaps there is a disturbance or a mishap in your daily routine. Something that may ruffle your feathers, misleading your intentions. There may be something that you see as an obstacle, when in fact if you begin to open your mind, and "feel" what it is that's happening around you, you begin to view and interpret situations differently. It's looking at each situation with wondrous eyes, to see beyond these obstacles.

Opportunities are swimming all around you every day. They may come to you in very subtle ways, such as a flutter or a change in the beating of your heart. You may see a photograph, or be engaged in a conversation, and a light goes on in your head. That's when you can activate and use your intuition, and let it help influence you when making decisions or choices. Be ready to launch yourself forward, at any given time and take advantage of these special circumstances. With an open mind, there lies ahead; a beautiful life with endless possibilities.

On a final note — don't run away with your imagination, pay close attention what you "feel". With clarity and balance, keep an open mind and an open heart so you can implement your visions. Seize every opportunity; as each opportunity will provide you with choices.

Ponder *—I see clearly that there is a path to endless*
opportunities in my life, which leads me to self-greatness —
Can I see opportunity through adversity or obstacles?
How can I clear my thought process so I can
recognize disguised opportunities?
Can I look at each situation with wondrous eyes?

"When an opportunity comes knocking —
See it through wondrous eyes.
Don't label the task or make excuses —
don't see it as an obstacle — don't fear it —
Instead — embrace it."

— Dr. Jill Lee *—*

Materialism isn't True Happiness

More isn't always better. We all tend to have this false sense of security when we have lots of "stuff" or lots of material assets. Have you ever asked yourself…"Who am I…the person?" Who are you without all your tangible assets? Is it really your possessions that make you happy or give you power? There is always a possibility that these "things" can be taken from you at any time. How do you think your life might be with less? Would it change who you are?

I'm not saying that material things aren't nice to have and that you should live without or not to enjoy what you do have. However, I am saying that there is too much importance given to what we have, instead of who we are. Again, ask yourself." Do I love? Am

I generous? Am I genuine? Am I passionate?" These are human qualities that matter most and can bring you happiness. Wouldn't you rather be admired and respected for who you are, not what you have?

Materialism can sometimes fill a void in life. Perhaps you feel deprived. Maybe it's a distraction from what may be going on in your personal world. It creates instant gratification; a kind of "quick fix" when you're feeling down. And we are all prone to comparing what we have to what others have and worrying how that reflects on ourselves. That fact is; that's the perfect recipe for stress, anxiety and frustration and can lead to unhappiness. That's your "false sense of security".

There are more important things in life than material assets. Nontangible assets like generosity, kindness and compassion to name a few. These are the things that lead to happiness. These are the personal assets that can be with you always and define the real you. They will bring instant gratification; not only to you but to others. These are riches that can never be purchased.

Find that balance of contentment in your life. Accept what is beneath your dreams and desires and let that move you forward. Challenge yourself in knowing who you are in the raw; in this material world, we live in. You may be pleasantly surprised with what you discover about yourself. Acquire things that money cannot buy and remember that nothing from the outside can give you what you need on the inside.

Ponder — *I see clearly that I create my true happiness,*
which comes from within —
Can the things that I a quire really give
me a sense of security?
Who am I without my material assets?
Do I love enough? Am I genuine and compassionate?

"Live, laugh, and love…for you are not
defined by the things you own.
Happiness cannot be purchased in a store."

— DR. JILL LEE —

WEEK THIRTY-THREE

Stepping Outside of Your Comfort Zone

We all seem to be wired to live within our comfort zone. It's part of human nature. This is a place where we feel safe, protected and in control. It's a place that minimizes stress or uncomfortable challenges. But it's also a place where you can become complacent or bored; where your growth is stifled. Stepping out of your comfort zone, like any other change in life, is a learned behavior.

What lies beyond this sacred space we have created for ourselves? There is an entire world, most often not tapped into. There lies exciting new challenges and opportunities for growth. Each and every day; outside your comfort zone is where all the magic and joy of life begins.

Stepping outside of your comfort zone may be difficult at first, bringing a bit of anxiety or fear. It's okay because you're exchanging the human habits and patterns of your everyday life, for change. You are expanding your physical and emotional state of being and perhaps entering an unfamiliar territory. But it's said that if you want something you've never had, you must do things you have never done. Learning to expand your thinking patterns is where change begins.

Meet each new challenge with a different mindset, bringing awareness to where your comfort levels are. Begin with slow and set conscious intentions. Know what inspires you and go for it one step at a time. See and reach beyond those horizons. Get creative and change the way you think. Acknowledge any anxiety or fears you may encounter and ask yourself… *"How difficult can it be?"* or *"What's the worst that can happen?"*

Taking risks can get your creative juices flowing while building character. The further you step outside your comfort zone the easier in time it becomes. You may even become more productive with existing tasks. Don't assume the outcome or let the fear of failure hold you back. Don't worry about what others may think or say. That alone can be your biggest obstacle.

Power up your inner forces and take risks. Remember that nothing is permanent and nothing is forever. Most often you can reverse your choices or decision, and chalk it up as experience. *"I tried it… I liked it…or not."* Life doesn't offer you guarantee's, but if you don't try something new, you'll never know what you may be missing.

Establish new habits and new life patterns that feel good and bring excitement into your life. It's time to get out of your own way. What's holding you back?

***Ponder** — I see clearly that each step I take out*
of my comfort zone brings new opportunities —
What is holding me back from stepping away
from what I know as "comfortable?"
Can I see beyond my fears with each new challenge,
to perhaps take a new direction?
Can I channel the excitement inside
to make bolder choices?

"As you step out of your comfort zone,
the joy of life will bring you new comfort."

— Dr. Jill Lee —

Daydreaming – It's Okay

Daydreaming is a fountain of thoughts streaming into a state of consciousness. Yes, even though your mind wanders; it's a place where you can enter your own internal world. Daydreaming allows you to visualize and go to a place you want to be. It's a beautiful head space that lets you detach yourself for a few moments and allows you to encounter beautiful thoughts about your future while you are still awake.

There is a part of your brain that controls these daydreams; not to be confused with your mind. As your mind is the activity of the brain. How you think depends on the brain's structure. Things are always changing and so goes your thoughts. Not to mention the nerve cells in your brain as you learn new things or encounter changes around you. Scientists have discovered that when the mind is not concentrating on a particular task, it can go into daydream mode.

People who daydream are often labeled as "spaced out", "non-productive' or even "unfocused". Big misconception! Daydreaming actually makes you more creative. It gives you insight and wisdom to things you may never have considered. You can imagine new possibilities that you never thought possible; bringing enthusiasm to a new project or anticipating positive results of an existing project. Daydreaming can be one of the most important techniques in achieving your goals.

Here are some positive effects daydreaming can have on your mindset:

Daydreaming:

- Helps you to visualize and see the end results or outcome of a project or situation

- Boosts creativity; helping you to achieve your goals

- Alleviates or relieves boredom

- It's a temporary escape from a stressful or burdensome task

- Helps your mind relax; giving you a "time out"

- Helps you organize your thoughts

- Brings you peace and serenity

So remember: Daydreaming helps you get the most out of your brain power. It's an essential resource for coping with life. It takes you away for a few moments; from where you are, to where you want to be. Daydreams…it's only a place to visit…not to live.

***Ponder** — I see clearly that I can use
daydreams to enhance my reality —
Can I allow myself the time to daydream?
How can I use my daydreams to be more creative?
Can I use my daydreams to bring clarity
when organizing my thoughts?*

*"Daydreaming is personal and belongs to only you
No one can ever take it from you
— Sweet Daydreams —."*

— DR. JILL LEE —

WEEK THIRTY-FIVE

Define Your Priorities

Will it take a personal crisis or a traumatic event for you to realize what you really value? Sadly, so often it does. Sometimes you just need to pause; open your heart and assess what your mind already knows.

Discovering your priorities is a personal task. It's not something that anyone can help you with. You might start by asking yourself a few questions like "What do I want my life to look like?" or "How do I want to spend my time"? You may even ask "Who do I want to spend my time with"? So many questions to ask, and that's where you begin; because only you hold the answers. You get to decide what is most important to you.

Once you sit and analyze your life situation, you start to discover that what you thought was so important, suddenly becomes so insignificant in the grand scope of things. It's easy to put so much emphasis on material "stuff" which can easily be gone in the blink of an eye. This is where the discovery and priorities come in. "What are my values?" "What are my gifts?"

Life can sometimes look like a puzzle with pieces that don't fit. But eventually piece by piece, you put it together. There is no short cut. There are no quick fixes and no tricks. Piece by piece it's all about you. When you ask and answer the above questions, only then can you start to prioritize what's most important in your life. You can then begin to manage your time, so you will have the luxury of taking advantage of incredible opportunities that may come your way. You become more productive with each task because you know what lies ahead. You will be able to enjoy the things you love. You can also create and take advantage of "play time" so you can enjoy everything in your life.

Try to utilize your time wisely, as time passes quickly. Days past… you can never have again. Know your values and prioritize them so you can enjoy what you have and what life has to offer.

Ponder — *I see clearly that I must prioritize my time,*
so I can enjoy each moment lived —
Do I know what I want my life to look like?
How can I shift and manage my schedule
so I can enjoy more free time?
What are the things that matter most important in my life?

"Search your heart and assess your priorities
before you embark on a new journey, realizing that
change and choice occur from the inside out."

— DR. JILL LEE —

WEEK THIRTY-SIX

Don't be Manipulated by Others

Have you ever felt like you were being controlled, taken advantage of, or manipulated by someone? Well, the fact is; the ones who manipulate and control do this merely because they can and because it works. You can even call this a form of emotional or psychological abuse. It violates your free-will and disrupts your well-being. This type of behavior can victimize, even humiliate you, breaking down your self-confidence. These people are most often narcissistic and self-absorbed, needing to be in control. They take advantage of others' weaknesses or vulnerabilities every chance they get. This can be quite exhausting and draining, and can even become expensive experience.

And you may ask how this is being done? Sometimes it's done in a very subtle way, and you may not even realize it's happening. Other times they can be quite bold. Perhaps they create an urgency or importance to a situation. They may threaten or bully you, even guilting you into doing something against your better judgment. This is how they gain control over their victims. Power is their food, and that's how they thrive. They just seem to know how to detect weakness and gravitate towards those who are most vulnerable.

Here are some ways you take back control of your life:

- Strengthen your weaknesses, and don't be naïve.

- Be direct and assertive to let your feelings be known.

- Learn to say no and walk away without feeling guilty. (You do this by giving value to your accountability and giving credit to yourself.)

- Stand up for yourself, and know that you matter.

- Stay true to your core values.

- Never compromise your integrity or self-respect.

- Set personal boundaries.

- Trust yourself and your instincts.

This behavior is not always intentional, but if allowed, it will continue. If this is something you have experienced, it's time to take a stand and disable it. You can set yourself free from the manipulations of others, by first becoming aware of those your associate yourself with and their intentions. Don't make yourself an easy target. Remember that the power of persuasion is and immense power of influence and we all have it. Use it wisely, so you can enrich your life, as well as the lives of others.

This is your life, your time. Don't let anyone hold you back from living your best life.

Ponder — *I see clearly that I am in control*
of my life and my choices.
How can I be more assertive and speak up for myself?
Can I recognize when someone is trying to manipulate me?
How can I strengthen my weaknesses?

"Identify and understand the difference between
persuasion and emotional manipulation.
Others may try to coerce you into an emotional
situation to suit their need — not yours —
This behavior only works when there is an audience —
keep your awareness alert."

— DR. JILL LEE —

Things we May Lose Sight Of

As humans, we are all wired the same, and we are all drawn to the mysterious unknown phenomena of life while seeking an adventure. We take our daily experiences and use them to move forward in life. But while searching for these wondrous adventures, it's so easy to miss something or lose sight of what life presents to us. The little things.

There are things in life that seem so insignificant to most people, such as notes in a song or the way words are printed on the page of a book. The fragrance and colors of the flowers in the garden and how the birds sing. How tall the tree has become that was planted in your front yard. Even the scent of one's cologne or perfume. These are just little things that we often pay no attention to in our day to day life. Why is that? Is it because it doesn't matter or is it because it may have no relevance to our daily existence? Well, all of these little things are part of your journey in life, and can make life a bit more interesting. These small things can help you to capture what is really in your heart. It's about becoming aware of what's in front of you… in the present moment.

When you have this stillness and quiet moments, you can reflect. Fond memories of your childhood come back and become clear and vivid. Colors seem brighter and more brilliant. You can hear the songs birds sing. You might even be able to hear the flowers dance. These little insignificant things can change the way you feel. You become more enthusiastic about life which can change what you may, in fact, be seeking. You suddenly see things differently. A smile comes to your face and perhaps a song in your heart. It's a matter of paying attention to what's in front of you, without clouded vision.

We sometimes need to pull back from the world around us. Find those moments of silence and just listen, see, remember, and feel. You're in charge of how you see and perceive each moment in your life. Know what is important to you. Life offers us all kinds of flavors. Find yours.

Ponder — *I see clearly that there may be little*
or insignificant moments in my life that I
should pay more attention to —
How can I make more time to stop and smell the roses?
Am I able to see all the flavors life has to offer?
Is there something I may be missing?
How can I bring more awareness to each step I take,
when embarking on a new adventure?

"Don't regret not seeing — don't regret not feeling —
Don't lose sight of what really matters."

— Dr. Jill Lee —

WEEK THIRTY-EIGHT

Being Present

By being present, I am not just talking about saying "I'm here". It's more about showing "You're here". Life itself is a miracle and is so often taken for granted. There is an internal connection you need, to get in touch with, that will help bring awareness to your everyday living. Understand your thoughts and emotions and take the initiative to eliminate doubts and disbeliefs you may be holding on to. Remind yourself of what is most important. Replace anything negative with something positive. Forgive, and forgive again. Don't hold on to grudges, for that only creates a God size hole in your heart that can never be filled.

To truly be present and available, you need to rid yourself of resentments, negative feelings, bad habits and the old ways of thinking. Look inside yourself with clear eyes and an open heart. Acknowledge and let go of what needs to be released. You might say it's just like cleaning your internal home. These are some of the things you must do to make yourself available. To be present.

If you want others to see you, then you need to show up. That means when you are with someone, a friend or loved one, you should give them your full attention. Perhaps even silent your mobile device. That shows them that they're important to you and that you are really listening to what they have to say. You are then "Being Present". It's all a matter of paying attention and being awake in the present moment. This simple cycle can profoundly change the way you experience life and your relationships as you know it.

Ponder — I see clearly that I must "show up and be
fully present" when communicating with others —
Am I holding unresolved resentment towards
another, that should be forgiven?
Do I have some "internal cleaning" that needs to be done?
How can I change some of my thinking patterns so
I can let go of what no longer serves my well-being?

"The past has no power to stop you
from being present now. Only your grievance
about the past can do that. What is grievance?
The baggage of old thought and emotion."

— Lao Tzu —

WEEK THIRTY-NINE

Self-Created Barriers

We sometimes hide behind a shield or a self- created barrier; not allowing anyone or anything to touch us. Not ever wanting to be hurt. We use these mental walls or barriers to block out thoughts that we may feel are not manageable. Thinking we have complete control and that we are protected or safe from any hurt or heartbreak. Well, life just doesn't work that way. Life situations have the "know how" to sneak in through the back door when we least expect it. We just never know from one moment to the next what may come our way or what challenges we may encounter.

Self-image and self-esteem issues can cause you to hide behind these barriers while, not allowing you to face your fears or situations, and only separating you from life and enjoying it. Learn to know and love your fate, whatever it may be. Most often there is a lesson to be learned and a path to be cleared. No experience is ever wasted.

In life situations, you don't often see the hidden message. The only way to hear or see those messages is for you to remove those barriers and let the mystery of life in. What's hiding behind your self-created barriers? What are you afraid to see or hear? Are there hidden emotions? Are there old wounds that need to be healed? Do you have misconceptions? Are you worried about what others may think? While all of these wonders go unanswered, you are missing out on living your best life. Illusion and separation must be replaced with clarity and openness.

Perhaps you need to free yourself from other people's expectations of you and start being who you are. Uncover your personal treasures layer by layer. Take those unexpected thoughts and emotions that go right up into your head and hide, and expose them. Become open enough to hear life's messages. Your mind can think and process things that separate you from reality and isolation. When you feel something tugging at you, find your interior silence, stop and pay attention. Don't hide. Find the courage to ask what lies in the bottom of your heart.

Give special attention to your emotions, as they hold great power. Although emotions come from your heart, sometimes they're right in front of your eyes and in front of your mind. Life has its own flow and its own logic. It's your responsibility to see how it works for you and how you can connect with each experience openly. Find that understanding and there are your rewards in life.

Ponder — *I see clearly that through self-esteem
and confidence, I can see my way through any
self-created barriers —
Do I need to pay more attention to my emotions?
What are they saying to me?
Can I see past other people's expectations of me?
What truly lies at the bottom of my heart?*

*"Open your heart and your mind. Don't allow yourself
to be held captive behind self-created barriers."*

— DR. JILL LEE —

FORTY

Creating Balance in Your Life

It's essential to our happiness that we all find balance in our lives. By living a more balanced life, greater energy goes into the goals you have set and, therefore, increases your productivity. It allows you the ability to be more focused on your daily tasks. When you are balanced, you have a sense that everything is streaming along, just as it should. You gain momentum with each project you tackle. It doesn't mean that everything is going to be perfect, it just means that you'll feel like you are able to accomplish more. You learn to recognize what works for you and what doesn't. Keynote…what doesn't work for you…change it!

What does balance look like to you? It's different for everyone. It's important not to try and do everything at once. Don't overwhelm yourself. Develop schedule and pace that works for you. All work and no play make for a very unhealthy lifestyle. So living a balanced life means that you must have time for work, time for play, you must have time for yourself.

Here are just a few suggestions you can try to schedule into your lifestyle to create that balance.

1   Learn to "turn it off."

Take a time away from your electronic devices, find some quiet time for yourself. Relax. This is probably the most important thing of all.

2   Treat yourself

Do something special for yourself, something that is just for you and you alone.

3   Expand your awareness

Perhaps finding some time to spend outdoors with nature. That can truly nurture you soul.

4   Create a social life

Find time to spend with people that have good energy and are fun to be with. People you can laugh with.

5   Create an efficient mindset

Get organized and write out a to-do list or a schedule.

6   Get rid of negative energies

Those negative energies are toxic to your health.

7   Pay attention to your health

Become aware of what your body is telling you. Then you have a balance of mind, body and soul.

We can't always anticipate and plan everything that's going to happen in our lives. But we can choose where to direct our energies. We can create a mindset that will allow us to live a well-balanced life.

***Ponder** — I see clearly that I must have balance
in my life. Time for work and time for play —
How can I address and let go of negative
energy that I may hold within?
Do I need to re-organize my schedule to create balance?
Can I turn off my mind so that I can enjoy "quiet time?"*

*"As you move throughout your day, find your pace.
Let any stress or drama pass through —
like a gentle breeze."*

— DR. JILL LEE —

Know Your Limits

Life itself; every day is a learning experience. Circumstances and situations occur; which causes life as you know it to shift. It may cause feelings to change, and that's okay. Sometimes we change out of necessity, sometimes out of desire.

Every situation, challenge or relationship has hidden messages, and it's up to you to figure out what they are and address each one of them. That's part of your self-awareness, which is essential to your everyday existence.

Knowing how and what you feel about any situation should be a priority in your life. Knowing what you have control over, and tuning into your feelings is also part of your self-awareness. Know your limits and what pushes your buttons or what stresses you out. By doing so, it allows you to set boundaries that work for you and setting those boundaries is a sign of self-respect.

When you are feeling uncomfortable in a situation, or you feel that someone has crossed the line with you, it shows a lack of respect on their part. It's okay to be direct and speak your mind, in a positive way and without feeling guilty about it. Give yourself permission to let them know where you draw the line and make them aware of your boundaries, respectfully. Remember that people are not mind readers, and your voice needs to be heard. If they can't respect your "space", then you may have to distance yourself from them. What good is a relationship of any sorts without respect anyway?

Setting boundaries is a skill and like any other skill, it requires practice. It's a process. You're not going to wake up one morning and have a new mindset ready to go. Take time and allow yourself to search deep in your heart, to hear what it's saying to you. Honor your feelings, and others will follow, with your direction.

Ponder — I see clearly that I must give myself
permission to create my personal boundaries —
Can I be more assertive and express to others
exactly what's on my mind?
If I am feeling uncomfortable in a situation,
how do I remove myself and take a different direction?
Can I move throughout the day and honor my feelings?

"Become the master of knowing your limits
and setting your boundaries."

— DR. JILL LEE —

Stop Playing Victim

There may be events or situations in our lives that cause us to "Play Victim". Sometimes we think that it empowers us and that we can manipulate someone or a situation. The fact is that it's just the opposite. When you act or behave like you have been victimized, you are actually becoming the oppressor. It's a trap so easily fallen into and most often self-inflicted. It's called "A Pity Party for One." This behavior hurts others, and its foundation is bitterness; which is like mental poison.

You may ask how can this hurt others? Well, it's a selfish act. It can suppress the feelings of others who really need a sympathetic or empathetic ear. Someone to listen and understand what they may be going through. It's not always about you! How different would your life be if you stopped validating those feelings of being a victim? You might start to like how you feel. You can become the one who helps a real victim.

So, how do you stop? It's a process. It's a habit that takes practice to change. It starts by looking within and realizing what's caused you to feel this way to begin with. Who is in charge of your soul? Perhaps you need to forgive someone who once hurt you. Forgiveness is a sign of strength, and that alone can give you internal power, therefore, not needing to play the victim. Once you learn to forgive, you can move away from the situation that hurt you. "Exit Pity Party."

You take control of your life. You choose where you want to be and who you want to spend your time with. You are in charge of your soul. You own your life. Learn to assume responsibility for everything in your life. You don't need to blame others. When you are faced with obstacles or challenges, you do something about it. Having a negative outlook on everything only creates more drama, and ultimately there you are…always the victim. So start by setting mini goals or quests for yourself. One day at a time, one event at a time. Think before you act on a situation. This helps you develop a healthier self-image and a better outlook on life in general. Learn to grow from negative situations; there is a lesson inside ever one of them; don't waste the message. Have the wisdom to turn a bad situation into power and stop getting stuck in the blame game. This is all part of taking responsibility for your life. Remember that "change" begins with you!

***Ponder** — I see clearly that when a situation
turns unpleasant, I can choose to leave
and exit the "Pity Party" —
How can I take responsibility for my actions
and not fall prey to becoming the victim?
What internal tools to I have to empower myself?
Can I be more empathetic to others,
and listen without judgment?*

*"Stand tall and believe in yourself —
for that is what truly matters."*

— DR. JILL LEE —

WEEK FORTY-THREE

The Importance of Slowing Down

Have you ever sat down and thought about special moments in time you may have missed because you were rushing around, or you didn't pace yourself? I bet there were many. Or perhaps the day seemed to fly by, and everything was just a blur? Does life seem to be on "high speed" and without a speed dial? It may feel that way, but the truth is, there is a "speed dial" and you own it. You are in control.

I know there are some things in life, we don't have the luxury of pacing, like parenting, work responsibilities, and school. But, for the most part, we have control over our schedules, and we also have the ability to regulate our time, as well as the pace in which we move.

Living in overdrive not only takes its toll on your physical body but also your mind. It invites stress and anxiety. You also become less productive and easily distracted. There may even be a change in your behavior and sleep patterns.

I am sure you have often heard the phrase "Stop and smell the roses." Well, the key word here is "stop". If you find yourself flustered, agitated, scattered or rushed, take a step back and "breathe." This will remind you that you are caught up in the busyness of that moment. By slowing down, or pausing for a moment, allows you to regroup and start again. You then become more productive and able to accomplish your tasks more efficiently.

Make time to rest. I know that may sound like a foreign word, but it is clear English. If even for a few moments throughout your day, pausing will bring you into a present time. It affords you the luxury to set your priorities, and perhaps re-organize your schedule. It's so easy to miss out on the things that matter most, moments that can never be replaced, by trying to do it all.

Learning to pace yourself takes mindfulness and practice. You may start by asking yourself… "Have all those seconds, minutes, hours, days, weeks, months, and years that you are living, are they being spent the best way possible?" Perhaps it's time to make adjustments.

Remember that time passed can never be recaptured. Time passed, fades the colors in your life, leaving only shadows, filling you with absent memories.

Ponder — *I see clearly that if I slow down and pace myself,*
I am less likely to miss out on special moments in my life,
that can never be recaptured —
Am I able to use my internal "speed-dial" to slow down?
How can I manage and adjust my schedule,
so that I pace myself and become completely present?
Am I using my time wisely?

"Time alone passes quickly enough on its own —
Slow down, feel and remember how it feels."

— DR. JILL LEE —

Raise Your Vibration

Your vibration is simply your overall state of being, aka your energy. Your being is composed of a variety of vibrations. Your thoughts, your emotions, your physical and mental frequencies vibrate at different levels, and everything in the Universe is made up of these energies.

You can sometimes associate your moods, emotions and your overall mental state with low energy levels; therefore bringing negative thoughts to the forefront. The vibrations that you project are picked by and felt by others. It's as if you were a magnet. However — the good news is that you are in control; more than you may realize. You start by not blaming others for your shortcomings. Stop the complaining and raise your vibration so everything around you has positive energy.

Become more aligned with who you are. Create balance in your life and begin with self-love. You will feel lighter, happier and more energetic. There will be less judgment of others and less aggressive behavior; creating fewer conflicts.

So you might be asking yourself at this point *"what can I do to raise my vibration?"* There are so many things you can do. Here are a few suggestions to help. Remember that not everything works for everyone. Find what works for you and start to elevate your energy levels. Keep in mind that "like attracts like."

1   Find some time to spend outdoors, in nature. Take in the natural beauty all around you. It can be most exhilarating.

2   Keep your body moving — Find an exercise that works for you. You will be amazed at how it elevates your mood.

3   Light meditation can help, along with deliberate breathing exercises, which brings calm into your life, recharging your brain.

4   Create positive affirmations for yourself every day. Remind yourself that you are worthy of a beautiful life.

5   A random act of kindness will not only lift your spirits but will lift the spirits of others.

6   Become aware of what you are watching and listening to. The type of music you listen to or the news and movies you watch can definitely have an effect on you.

7   Drink plenty of water, as it flushes out toxins from the body, also increasing your energy levels.

Everything in this Universe is made up of energy; vibrating at different frequencies. We — as humans — have the ability to pick up the energy from others; good, bad, or indifferent. So be aware who you invite into your space.

Remember that life is a practice and any change you bring into your life takes time to perfect. Be patient with yourself, but be aware at the same time. Be alive in your life.

***Ponder** — I see clearly that I must be mindful*
of my thoughts and emotions, and the energy they put
out can be picked up by others —
What daily rituals can I incorporate into my day
so that I can elevate my energy?
Do I allow the vibrations of others to affect my well-being?
Do I have control over who I invite into my world
and who I wish to spend time with?

"Raise your vibration and create a healthier
and more positive lifestyle.
Cultivate and practice forgiveness —
compassion — gratitude — and empathy —
And love — always, unconditionally."

— Dr. Jill Lee —

Coping with Toxic Family Members

I'm sure you've all heard the saying "You can choose your friends, but you can't choose your family". Well, technically, this may be true. However, you *can* choose who you invite into your circle and to be a part of your life. Some people happen to be very lucky and enjoy the relationships with their family while others may find it painstakingly difficult to be around them.

Just because you share the same bloodline, doesn't mean that you are going to grow up and be the best of friends. As we develop into adults, people change, as do our relationships…and for many different reasons. But the reasons don't really matter. As drama unfolds, it can be like being in the midst of a storm. The point is, if the relationship becomes dysfunctional, explosive, or toxic, then it becomes necessary for you to part ways. This may apply to a sibling, a child, an aunt, uncle, or cousin, or even a parent. And then you have members of your family where you don't share the same genes, but perhaps they have become related through marriage, such as in-laws, (all the spouses of those previously mentioned) or even your spouse. The same also applies. I don't believe that the definition of family necessarily means friends.

Nobody has the right to violate you, in any way. When this happens, you need to give yourself permission to walk away, without guilt, without hate, but with dignity and self-respect. You don't need to pretend that their behavior is okay when it's not. Learn to untangle yourself from the family drama. Learn to set boundaries. Know that just because they hold the title of family, doesn't give them the right to be a part of your life. That is something that must be earned through mutual respect. The relationship must be a win-win for everyone, or it doesn't work at all.

When you walk away, you may find that other relationships in your family may become strained, because of the choices you have made. Some may see you as ruthless, selfish, or uncaring, but it really doesn't matter. What is important is your well-being. They must learn to accept your decisions and respect your choices. Remember, what's good for one is not always good for everyone.

Stay true to your core values and know that there are some relationships that can never be repaired or mended. The mere presence of some people is just not healthy for your state of mind. You can't possibly place a value on your sanity.

It may take some time to heal from these separations. Surround yourself with positive people and with those who can share mutual love and respect. Recognize the signs and establish new personal boundaries. It's your responsibility to protect your personal space, your world, and your well-being.

__Ponder__ — I see clearly that nobody has the right
to violate me in any way —
How do I take the responsibility
to protect my personal space?
Can I walk away from a family member and set
boundaries when I feel that I have been disrespected,
violated or the relationship has become dysfunctional?
How important is my state of well-being and my sanity?

Removing toxic people from your life is essential
in maintaining a peaceful state of mind."

— Dr. Jill Lee —

What You Allow — Will Continue

What you allow is what will continue in your life, seems to be a simple concept to identify with; however it's not always an easy concept to address. Through all of our relationships, personal and professional, and with all the people we encounter in our lives, we are able to see and experience different behavior patterns. We try to surround ourselves and develop those relationships with those that are kind and loving; those who think much the same as we do. That's a nice scenario — right? Well, you know as well as I do, that that's not always the case. There may come a time when these conflicts may cause you to make the most difficult choices you have ever had to make.

Often we become comfortable in certain situations or relationships because it may be easier just to grit our teeth and accept what is. It may just be part of your nature to be kind, polite, empathetic and cordial. There are other times when you may become frustrated with a situation, and conflict arises, and that someone has touched on your last nerve. What do you do? How do your react? You walk away and say "Oh…That's just how she/he is" or, on the flip side, you walk away sad, hurt, and with a bruised heart. You may even make an excuse for how you are being treated. You fall victim to these toxic behavior patterns, by allowing their negative behavior and energy to become infested in your mind, disrupting your inner-peace.

Examine and measure what you tolerate. Then decide at what point do you stop allowing others to take advantage of your kindness, your good nature, and your generosity? Be in charge of what you want, and who you allow in your life. Sometimes you have to step back, detach your emotions and let others take responsibility for their own negative actions. We don't have control over others, but we do have control over the life within ourselves, as well as our choices. We can choose not to engage in other people's negativity,

Be reminded that we teach others how to treat us, by what we accept or allow. Ask yourself… *"What needs to stop? What needs to change? Does this work for me? Does it serve my well-being?"* Be reminded of your self-worth and you will regain your self-respect, as well as the respect of others.

Ponder — *I see clearly that I teach others how
to treat me, by the behavior I tolerate and accept —
At what point to I put my foot down
and say "enough is enough?"
Can I recognize when someone is trying to
take advantage of my good nature?
Can I take a step back, remove my emotions for the
moment, and evaluate a relationship or situation to
recognize what's best for my well-being?*

*"Don't fall victim to the behavior of others —
you always have a choice."*

— Dr. Jill Lee —

Filling an Empty Heart Space

Have you ever had that feeling of emptiness? A sense that your insides are like a bottomless pit? Many people hold on to the emptiness inside, because then don't know how to fill that space. It starts when you abandon yourself; by holding judgment and not honoring your inner guidance.

You may have experienced the loss of a loved one. You may be engaging in an unsatisfying relationship, or you may be feeling rejection. Perhaps there are financial struggles or even boredom. All of these mentioned can be symptoms or beliefs that cause you to have an empty heart. Truth be told…these are beliefs and temporary at that.

I use the word "beliefs" because although these are situations you've encountered, you have the ability to change how you are affected. How…you might ask? Emptiness does not come from the lack of something external but rather the lack of something internal.

You may try to fill this empty space with substances like food, drugs or alcohol. You may engage in purchasing material things. Do you really believe that material things will fill the empty space in your heart? Through all of this, the emptiness still exists. These are just temporary fillers, and there will still be something still tugging at your heart.

The key is to listen and honor your internal voice; which comes from your spirit. Take responsibility for your inner being — emotionally, mentally and spiritually. Find what ignites your spirit and don't repress any emotions. When you know a passion so spectacular — so amazing — so immense — you will realize you no longer feel empty.

There is no Fairy Godmother with a magic wand; you must seek what your heart desires from within. Seek what you love. Love is always there to fill your heart when your heart is open. When your heart is closed, you become a prisoner of your own emptiness.

Ponder — *I see clearly that I am in control of filling any empty space in my heart —*
How can I release my emotions and listen immensely to what my heart is telling me?
What is it that ignites the passion I have within?
How do I unlock my passions so I am no longer a prisoner to the emptiness?

"When you know a passion so spectacular —
so amazing — so prodigious —
A passion that ignites your spirit —
feel it in the deepest depths of your soul —
don't repress the emotion it brings —
Let it tear your heart wide open and live that passion."

— Dr. Jill Lee —

WEEK FORTY-EIGHT

The Need to Control

Are you aware that your need to control others can be compromising your relationships? It can also keep you from living in the present, and enjoying your life because you become consumed with the outcome of other people's circumstances. *"Control" is a need.* A need for a sense of certainty, by attaching yourself to an outcome. The need to know what's going to happen next or what will happen if…Perhaps trying to insist that someone else see your point of view.

Being controlling creates a false sense of power. It becomes easy for you to be misunderstood and can change the context of any situation. You may even find yourself interfering in someone's personal business. Others may see it as if you're trying to alter their thoughts or redefining their reality, leaving them to feel incredibly insecure and uncomfortable. Trying to control another person; is actually a form of manipulation.

Why such a need to control? Sometimes it comes from jealousy, insecurity, a reaction to fear or emotional distress, just to mention a few. The fact is; that you only have control over what is in your mind and control over your own physical actions.

Once you become mindful of this type of behavior, you can start letting it go. Take a step back and analyze your situation. Create new patterns for yourself. Allow others to succeed or to make their own mistakes. Maybe refrain from giving advice. You may be able to influence others instead of controlling them; simply by your kindness.

You may be uncomfortable at first with this new behavior. You may feel inadequate or that you are letting others down by, not giving your advice. Stop fighting with yourself. It takes great internal discipline. But fear not, the best way to love others is to let them be who they are. Be a part of their life, not in control of it.

Ponder — *I see clearly that "control" is a need.
I know that I only have control over myself —
Can I take a step back and allow others to
make their own mistakes?
How do I create new behavior patterns and
restrain from giving unsolicited advice?
How do I let go of the notion that I need to
control others or a situation?*

*"Letting go of control doesn't mean that you don't care.
It means that you realize you only have control over yourself."*

— DR. JILL LEE —

WEEK FORTY-NINE

Shift Your Negative Thoughts

Do you realize that your thoughts control your life? Yes, your thoughts can shape your life. When you hold negative thoughts, you make life much more difficult than necessary. Negative thoughts hold you back from accomplishing and achieving your goals. They can also sabotage your relationships as well as your happiness. Negative thoughts can draw you down and bring others along with you. They can also result in careless or impulsive life choices.

Negative thoughts can also become excuses, which often, are manifested by overthinking or assuming, causing you to imagine the worst and magnifying your manifestations. And sometimes it's easy to slip into a *"woe is me"* syndrome. *"I'm not good enough"*, *"Nothing ever works out for me"*, *"I can't"*, or a number of other negative speculations. How about *"It's too hard"*? Do any of these quotes sound familiar? These are thoughts and assumptions that can hold you hostage, which in turn restricts you from enjoying your desired life.

Your thoughts, negative as well as positive, have tremendous power. You are in control; therefore, you can change, shift, or modify your thoughts at any time. Acknowledge and release the negative intentions, in exchange for new and positive thinking patterns. Counter the negative thoughts with positive affirmations. Learn to step back, relax into it and ask yourself, *"Is there validity to this negative thought?"*

We are all confronted and visited by negativity. If it touches you, try not to allow it to consume you or settle inside. When you shift these thoughts, everything around you suddenly appears different — lighter — and your life begins to flow with ease and clarity. You can't expect to have a positive life when you hold on to negative thoughts.

Don't judge the future by your past. Stop blaming yourself for mistakes that may have occurred. Every challenge or life situation is a lesson learned. Continue to dream big, and move towards your future one step at a time.

When you change the way you think, when you look at the positive, you can then visualize the outcome of your desired life. Yes, change the tone of your thoughts. This takes effort, time, and practice. Now is the time for you to take responsibility; you can create and design the life you desire to live.

Ponder — *I see clearly that my thoughts control my life.*
I live what I think, and think what I live —
How can I change the tone of my thoughts
to live the life that I desire?
Am I able to see hidden lessons in mistakes
or poor choices I may have made?
Can I let go of the past and any mistakes
or blunders I may have made?

"Positive thoughts, happy thinking, brings a happy life."

— DR. JILL LEE —

Find Your Happy Place

Does this scenario sound at all familiar? It's time to start the day. Wake up and rush to get out of the house, only to sit in traffic while on your way to work. You finally arrive, and you're confronted with obligations and challenges of the day. In the midst of it all, anxiety develops and stress sets in. Time to go home and yep! …more traffic after a tough day at the office. You get home, and the stress of the day still resides inside you. Dinner time, maybe some homework, and if you're lucky; perhaps a little R&R or television time. Then it's off to bed, only to wake up tomorrow and do it all over again. It seems to be that we are always stuck in a hurry to get somewhere or to do something.

Have you ever asked yourself… *"Is that all there is?"* Well, the answer is **NO!** Life has so much to offer when you take the time to calm your mind and find your "Happy Place." You might be asking yourself

"Just where is this "Happy Place" and how do I get there?" Believe it or not, you don't have to go very far because it resides within.

You may feel you don't have the time, or that obstacles are holding you back. You may even feel that you are undeserving. *Not So!* Everyone has a "Happy Place" and it's different for each one of us. Some find it through physical exercise or activities while others find it in a quiet environment. Some may find it through a favorite vacation spot or just spending time with those you love. You can even go there, through your own happy thoughts. *Dr. Bamblings* says, *"Happiness is about contentment or general dispositions rather than a destination."* That is precisely the point. It doesn't matter where you find it, as long as it's found. Make time to do what you love. Smile, laugh and play as often as you can.

Like any other behavior pattern, it is a learned and practiced mindset. You train your mind to notice what it is that makes you happy, and you go there. So close your eyes and calm your mind. Visualize and feel your "Happy Place." Hold on to that vision and go there as often as you can. Honor what feeds your soul. Set your intentions, as manifestation creates reality. And that's how you find your "Happy Place."

Ponder — *I see clearly that I have a "Happy Place"*
and it resides within. Happiness is not a destination;
it's part of by everyday journey —
Do I know how to define my "Happy Place?"
How can I modify my thinking habits to
quiet the chatter in my mind?
Can I start each morning with a new ritual by setting
positive and direct intentions?

"You've been given this gift of "now."
Simply and effortlessly embrace this time
Know where your "Happy Place" is, and be there."

— DR. JILL LEE —

Forgiving

To forgive doesn't always mean to forget. It doesn't mean that you don't feel, it doesn't mean the situation never happened. It doesn't mean that you give the other person a pass or pardon, and it certainly doesn't mean that you must keep this person in your life.

What it does mean, is that you are making a conscious choice to let go of resentment and anger. It's like giving yourself a gift. You are putting a seal on the situation, which brings closure and gives you the strength to move on.

To forgive is not always such an easy task. There may be situations that are so very painful; you wonder how it is ever possible to forgive, or a sense of righteousness that holds you back from forgiving. You must set aside your pride as well as your ego, take a deep breath

— and then ask yourself — *"What do I gain by holding on to this grudge? How will I feel once I have forgiven?"* Once you have the answers, the healing process can begin. Only when you clear away these emotional toxins from your heart, can you forgive freely.

The act of forgiveness of oneself is equally important. As humans, we all make mistakes or have regrets for something we've done to hurt another. Without self-forgiveness, your guilt will only fester. Acknowledge your mistake, and ask yourself — *"What have I learned from my mistake? How can I make it better? Can I make better choices?"* It's all part of letting go of the past, and moving forward. You cannot move on when you are burdened with suppressed guilt.

Your mental health depends on your ability reduce hurt and anger aimed towards others as well as yourself.

***Ponder** — I see clearly that forgiveness is a gift to myself —*
Can I acknowledge my mistakes and forgive myself
for any wrongdoings I may have done?
How can I "right" any "wrongs" that may have occurred?
Can I forgive others, but not forget,
and still let go of the hurt?

"When you forgive — forgive from your heart —
and without expectations."

— Dr. Jill Lee —

WEEK FIFTY-TWO

As The Year Ends, There Are New Beginnings

"Auld Lang Syne" is a poem written by Robert Burns in 1788. These words are sung to a folk tune; a tradition used to bid farewell to the year ending at the stroke of midnight. Meaning…times long past, according to the description from *Wikipedia:" It's a reminder to all of us that newness is about to begin."*

So as we bid this year adieu, we should all stop; take the time to pause and reflect. Ask yourself…"What's definitive about this year end? Is it time for healing and closure? Is it time for new beginnings? It's the perfect opportunity to recall lessons learned throughout the year.

As we take this time to reflect, not dwell, we open our minds to clear the way for new visions and new opportunities. We are reminded

141

of what's most important in our lives. Your mind, body, soul, and spirit are all connected and already know what's meant to be kept and what should be released; knowing where there is excess or deficiencies. So listen to your inner guidance and wisdom telling you what needs to emerge, so you can make life better for yourself and those around you.

Again, take the time to know what your needs are and what makes your spirit come alive; what rejuvenates your soul. Only then can you banish your fears, doubts, and worries to make room for dreams, aspirations and joy.

It's time to think about the New Year and what you would like to accomplish. Begin to set new goals, created by your clear intentions. Consider setting short-term goals so that you can enjoy a sense of achievement. Become aware and be mindful, as this will bring balance into your life.

Look forward to this New Year and seize every opportunity. Open your inside door and move forward with clarity, strength, confidence, and determination. Make this coming year the best year ever!

Ponder — *I see clearly that I must seize every opportunity*
that comes my way. I believe in myself —
What is the most important lesson
that I have learned this year?
What would I most like to accomplish this coming year?
Do I have clarity? Have I transcended to self-reliance?

"Seek clarity so you will have a deep understanding
and appreciation of who you are;
your true value and self-worth.
Embrace gratitude and open your heart
so you can love and be loved.
Let there be stillness, so you can hear your heart speak."

— Dr. Jill Lee —

With Each Day — Seek Clarity

*Make the time to take a step back, pause,
and take a cleansing breath before moving forward
in making choices, decisions, or commitments.*

*Tune into your energy — listen and feel your intuition,
feel your vibrations.*

*Be wise enough to know what feels right —
and let that illuminate your soul.*

*Learn to rethink the beginning of your day —
Enjoy a brief moment of heartfelt sentiments.*

See clearly — how you would like the day to flow —

For the choices you choose today, will determine your life tomorrow.

— Sweet Blessings —

— Dr. Jill Lee —

My Reflection

Week One — Life is A Gift; Living is an Art

Date: _______________________________

____

____

____

____

Week Two — Listen to The Internal Callin of My Heart

Date: _______________________________

____

____

____

____

Week Three — Expext Unexpected Challenges

Date: ___________________________

____

____

____

____

Week Four — Remove Self-Created Illusions

Date: ___________________________

____

____

____

____

Week Five — The Effects of Chaos to Stress

Date: _______________________

____

Week Six — Learning to Cope

Date: _______________________

Week Seven — Manage My Emotions

Date: _______________________

____

____

____

____

Week Eight — Every Choice Has A Consequence

Date: _______________________

____

____

____

____

Week Nine — Inner-Strength and Self-Discipline: My Power Within

Date: _______________________________

____

____

____

____

Week Ten — Release My Negative Emotions

Date: _______________________________

____

____

____

____

Week Eleven — Change Promotes Growth

Date: _______________________________

____

____

____

____

Week Twelve — Expand My Personal Boundaries

Date: _______________________________

____

____

____

____

Week Thirteen — Knowing My True Self

Date: _______________________

____

____

____

____

Week Fourteen — Doubt My Doubts

Date: _______________________

____

____

____

____

Week Fifteen — Am I Settling?

Date: _______________________

____

____

____

____

Week Sixteen — Living With Integrity

Date: _______________________

____

____

____

____

Week Seventeen — Creative Mind Energy

Date: _______________________

____

____

____

____

Week Eighteen — Imperfection or Unique?

Date: _______________________

____

____

____

____

Week Nineteen — Live With Intent

Date: _______________________________

____

____

____

____

Week Twenty — Unclutter My Life

Date: _______________________________

____

____

____

____

Week Twenty-One — My Character

Date: _______________________

____

____

____

____

Week Twenty-Two — My Core Beliefs

Date: _______________________

____

____

____

____

Week Twenty-Three — Resolving Conflicts

Date: _________________________

____

____

____

____

Week Twenty-Four — Words Matter

Date: _________________________

____

____

____

____

Week Twenty-Five — Dealing With Dissapointment

Date: _______________________

____

____

____

____

Week Twenty-Six — Rise Above Advirsity

Date: _______________________

____

____

____

____

Week Twenty-Seven — My Peace, My Serenity

Date: _______________________________

____

____

____

____

Week Twenty-Eight — Needs vs. Desires

Date: _______________________________

____

____

____

____

Week Twenty-Nine — Letting Go of Guilt

Date: _______________________

Week Thirty — Ego

Date: _______________________

Week Thirty-One — Circumstances Brings Opportunities

Date: _______________________

____

____

____

____

Week Thirty-Two — Materialism Isn't Ture Happiness

Date: _______________________

____

____

____

____

Week Thirty-Three — Stepping Outside of My Comfort Zone

Date: _______________________

Week Thirty-Four — Daydreaming – It's Okay

Date: _______________________

Week Thirty-Five — Define My Priorities

Date: _______________________________

____

____

____

____

Week Thirty-Six — I Won't Be Manipulated By Others

Date: _______________________________

____

____

____

____

Week Thirty-Seven — Things I May Lose Sight of

Date: _______________________________

____

____

____

____

Week Thirty-Eight — Being Present

Date: _______________________________

____

____

____

____

Week Thirty-Nine — Self Created Barriers

Date: _______________________________

____

____

____

____

Week Forty — Creating Balance In My Life

Date: _______________________________

____

____

____

____

Week Forty-One — Know My Limits

Date: _______________________________

____

____

____

____

Week Forty-Two — Stop Playing Victim

Date: _______________________________

____

____

____

____

Week Forty-Three — The Importance Of Slowing Down

Date: _______________________

____

____

____

____

Week Forty-Four — Raise My Vibration

Date: _______________________

____

____

____

____

Week Forty-Five — Coping With Toxic Family Members

Date: _______________________

____

____

____

____

Week Forty-Six — What I Allow – Will Continue

Date: _______________________

____

____

____

____

Week Forty-Seven — Filling My Empty Heart Space

Date: _______________________________

Week Forty-Eight — The Need To Control

Date: _______________________________

Week Forty-Nine — Shifting My Negative Thoughts

Date: _______________________

____

____

____

____

____

Week Fifty — Finding My Happy Place

Date: _______________________

____

____

____

____

Week Fifty-One — Forgiving

Date: _______________________

____

____

____

____

**Week Fifty-Two — As The Year Ends
There Are New Beginnings**

Date: _______________________

____

____

____

____

*"With clarity, you have the ability to create balance
and harmony in your life —
It's about turning "I can't" into "I can" —
It's about catch and release —
It's about holding on to what matters most —
And letting go of what no longer serves your well-being —
It's about transcending to self-reliance"*

— DR. JILL LEE —

DR. JILL LEE

As a wife, mother, and grandmother, life has offered me an abundance of unimaginable experiences as well as my share of challenges.

I have also been a business owner for over 40 years and have worked with people from all around the world and from all walks of life. Self-taught and diversified in every aspect of my manufacturing business, I learned it all from the ground up. I have interfaced with companies that were just starting out in business to some of the largest mega-corporations in the world.

One of the greatest rewards for me over the years, was the opportunity to work with hundreds of loyal employees and thousands of clients. Every day brought a new challenge, and I was there, not only with an open ear but with an open heart. It is through these experiences that I had discovered my passion for working with others; to help bring balance, clarity, and harmony into their lives.

I then made a choice to take my life into a new direction and follow my passion. I became a Certified Holistic Life Coach, and earned my Ph.D. in Philosophy, as well as becoming an Ordained Reverend. With a thirst for knowledge, I couldn't stop there. I studied and received my Certification in Crystal Therapy and Crystal Healing.

It is now with great passion that I work with many individuals and their families who have life-altering situations and challenges, or simply looking to change directions in their life. I help others discover their strengths and guide them in a direction, so they can flourish in their own light, and live their best life.

Dr. Jill Lee is available for Seminars,
Keynotes, and Retreats, based on her book;

Fifty-Two Weeks of Clarity: How to Transcend to Self-Reliance

Mail: Dr. Jill Lee — 2416 W Victory Blvd.
#122 — Burbank, CA 91506
Telephone: 1-818-859-6104
Email: *jill@lifecoachwithheart.com*
Web: *http://www.lifecoachwithheart.com/*
Facebook: *https://www.facebook.com/HearttoHearts1*

PGIL2021USA